WWE LEGENDS

BRIAN SOLOMON

Foreword by Sgt. Slaughter

World
Wrestling
Entertainment®
BOOKS

POCKET BOOKS
New York   London   Toronto   Sydney

For my grandfather, Anthony Salica

CONTENTS

DIRTY ROTTEN SCOUNDRELS:
THE FOLKS YOU LOVED TO HATE

IT'S ALL ABOUT PRIDE: ETHNIC IDOLS

U.S.A. IS NOT OKAY: THE FOREIGN MENACE

TOSSING IN TANDEM: THE TAG TEAM GREATS

BLAME IT ON RIO:
THE EARLY INTERCONTINENTAL CHAMPS

THE WEIRD AND THE WACKY

FOREWORD

In the long, glorious history of World Wrestling Entertainment, there have been many incredibly gifted and legendary athletes, but only a select few have ever received the upright distinction of being called legends. There is, however, a fine line between being a legend and being legendary. A legendary person is famous and popular. A legend is someone who inspires others and is looked up to by his peers not only for his accomplishments but for his success; not just for getting his picture on the cover of magazines and cereal boxes, or appearing in commercials and movies. A legend is only interested in and satisfied by results. He is not a politician, and he doesn't look to win a popularity contest. A legend is a one-of-a-kind, unique originator and motivator who is well respected by those before him for keeping open the road that he pioneered, and helps to pave it for others to follow. A legend is a born leader, whose hard work and dedication has given those presently making the journey the same opportunity to one day become legends themselves.

As a young fan of wrestling in the Midwest, World Wide Wrestling Federation was a place that I never knew much about. We did not get their shows in our region, and only knew about them from reading wrestling magazines. The American Wrestling Association was what I saw on TV when I was growing up. But after I got into the business of professional wrestling, I soon learned that World Wide Wrestling Federation was the mecca; it was the company that you wanted to work for one day. That's where all the big stars were, that's where the big money was. That's where you could become a legend.

Your goal—at least, it was mine when I first got into professional wrestling—was to some day get to New York City and work for WWWF. That was a young wrestler's dream. You would see the names, people like Killer Kowalski, Bobo Brazil, and Bruno Sammartino, and later on, Andre the Giant, Pedro Morales, Superstar Billy Graham, and Bob Backlund. It was the major league of professional wrestling. All the others were kind of minor league.

To be recognized as a legend, especially by WWE, the leader in sports entertainment, is a great honor and puts you in an elite class. However, the road to becoming a legend is not an easy one, and it involves many hardships and sacrifices. Not only do you work through injuries and illness, but you are constantly away from home, traveling countless miles on the road. Very seldom do you celebrate birthdays, anniversaries, or holidays with your family. Your time away from your loved ones, and their time without you, is very difficult. You could never achieve the title of legend without their love, their support, and an understanding of your passion.

Another strong characteristic of a legend is his ability to be a ring general, both inside and outside the squared circle. As an entertainer, you have to be able to feel the crowd, feel what the crowd wants, and give it to them. That's something you can't teach. It's something you're born with, an instinct. Being a ring general is like being an artist, a storyteller. Although there are still a few ring generals in today's world of sports entertainment, it is becoming a lost art. An audience wants to be told a story; they want to believe. And the reason they are there is to be entertained. Nothing more, nothing less. They want to cheer for the heroes and boo the villains, and your task as a performer—and what eventually determines your status as a legend—is your ability to feel and control your audience at each particular event, because each audience is different.

As a true master of entertainment, the ring general would have his audience in the palm of his hand before he would set one foot into the gladiatorial combat zone. He evaluated the attitude and emotions of his awaiting audience, especially if he was the villain—which is what many ring generals are, and the character most legends preferred to portray. Being the hero is a much more complicated, strenuous, and difficult personality to establish. Only a handful of legends have had the ability to grasp and enact the role of the beloved hero. A performance between a hero ring general and a villain ring general doesn't happen often, but when it does, it is truly a classic in the art of storytelling. One of those special and magical moments took place in 1981 at Madison Square Garden, in a battle called the Alley Fight between myself and Pat Patterson.

Another reason legends were held in such high esteem was their ability to fill venues to their capacity. There are no two greater words to hear, when you are in the main event at Madison Square Garden, the most famous building in sports history, than "SOLD OUT!" The only other words that come close, especially from your peers, are "Thank you." It is so important to remember the accomplishments and sacrifices the legends put forth for all of us who are in WWE today. If it wasn't for these people, who tried something different and wanted to develop this type of entertainment, it might not be here today. You have to remember that. It's wonderful to know those days are indeed still remembered. It means that those people were successes, that they truly were legends!

—Sgt. Slaughter

INTRODUCTION

**Before there was *WrestleMania*,
before there was *Hulkamania*,
there were WWE Legends. . . .**

The hundred-and-thirty-year-old American phenomenon most commonly known as professional wrestling has a rich and fascinating history. And perhaps no other entity in wrestling has a greater history than World Wrestling Entertainment. True to the forward-thinking philosophy that has made it the most powerful sports entertainment company on the planet, WWE is always hard at work promoting the next big event or the newest sensation. After all, the future is the lifeblood of the industry. As a result, there isn't always time to reflect on the past and the accomplishments of those who came before.

That's where *WWE Legends* comes in. Think of it as a time-out, a break from that forward momentum to take a look at those individuals who helped build WWE as we know it today, and have known it for much of the past two decades.

The purpose of this book is to celebrate the careers of forty of the most influential and important figures from WWE's early "territorial" period, ranging roughly from 1953 through 1983. The reason I have chosen to confine this book to that period is simple. In the last twenty years, WWE has become an international powerhouse, a cultural phenomenon whose Superstars are literally household names. Thanks to the mainstream promotional machine the company has become, today's fans are well aware of the exploits of men like Hulk Hogan, Roddy Piper, Randy Savage, Bret Hart, Shawn Michaels, Undertaker, Stone Cold Steve Austin, and The Rock. These legends were created during a time when WWE had taken the game over almost completely, and their stories have been well told many times over the years. Fans feel they know them inside out.

But what about those individuals who made their mark during the days when the company was but one of an array of regional territories spread out across North America? Those who spent the majority of their careers during a time when WWE was confined primarily to the northeastern United States, "from Maine to Maryland"? These are people whose stories are not as well known. These are the people who helped to build the foundation on which that later empire would be built. And these are the people whose lives are chronicled here.

I have chosen as the dividing line Hulk Hogan's January 23, 1984, Heavyweight Championship victory over the Iron Sheik. Although the company's national expansion had already been set in motion by that point, that title change was the symbolic changing of the guard, ushering in an entirely new era for the company and the business as a whole. The tradition of *WrestleMania*, the annual extravaganza that has become the Super Bowl of sports entertainment, would soon follow. The territorial days were over, and WWE was on the road to becoming something different from what it had been before. From UHF to Pay-Per-View, and from smoke-filled armories to the Pontiac Silverdome, the explosion was dramatic.

Therefore, in order to be included in this book, a performer is required to have been a major performer in WWE who made his name primarily, if not entirely, prior to the so-called modern era. In certain cases, individuals lingered on well into the *Hulkamania* era and even beyond, but their greatest moments took place earlier.

Other than that, what makes someone a "WWE Legend"? Quite simply, being a WWE Legend is different from being any other kind of wrestling legend. From the start, WWE was a unique organization, full of color and flamboyance. It took a lot more to make it there than it did anywhere else, and rightfully so, since it was the biggest and most successful territory in America. More than just knowing how to wrestle, you had to be a personality, someone who connected to the fans. You had to have charisma in abundance. No other organization took the entertainment aspect of the business to heart as much, which is why the company later renamed their product "sports entertainment." And that's why these legends are so unique. More than musty, dusty old faces from the past, they are all vibrant, unforgettable characters.

It's certainly not required that you lived through all this in order to enjoy this book. Rather, I hope it appeals to fans of many varieties. In fact, it probably will hold more interest for those not as well acquainted with wrestling history than those who are "authorities" on it. Maybe you're someone who doesn't know much about these folks but are interested, as I was, in finding out more about these names you've heard mentioned. Maybe you remember many of them from when you were younger and are looking to relive your past a little. Or maybe you've even lost touch with the business as it stands today, but still relish the memories of those greats of yesteryear. If any of these is the case, then this book is for you.

The concept behind *WWE Legends* began six years ago as an idea for a trading card set. However, WWE's ongoing partnership with Simon & Schuster created the opportunity to execute it on a much grander scale, one that would be able to do it justice. Much has changed since the beginning, specifically the list of legends itself—along the way, some tough choices were required.

In addition to the criteria already mentioned, I used other methods to narrow down the candidates. For example, many individuals who may have plied their trade in WWE before 1984 nevertheless achieved their greatest glory afterward, and were therefore disqualified. This is why people like Tito Santana, Big John Studd, Greg "The Hammer" Valentine, and Jesse "The Body" Ventura are not here. Also, performers who achieved the vast majority of their fame outside WWE were not included. This eliminates people who built their legacies primarily in other places, such as Dusty Rhodes

(Florida/Mid-Atlantic), the Sheik (Detroit), Ray Stevens (San Francisco/AWA), and Mil Mascaras (Mexico).

For each legend, I've made every attempt to provide "official stats." In the case of heights, weights, and hometowns, it's important to remember that this refers to the original promotional stats billed at the time the performer was active, which is why, for example, Ivan Koloff is listed as being from Moscow, Russia, even though his profile gives his birthplace as Canada. Since wrestling has always been about illusion, the "accuracy" of such stats will always be open to debate.

The use of the company's name may also be a source of confusion, and a brief history lesson is in order to help clear that up. In 1952, Vincent J. McMahon—father of current chairman Vincent K. McMahon—started up a company called the Capitol Wrestling Corporation, a member of the national body known as the National Wrestling Alliance (NWA). In 1963, Capitol broke away from the NWA and created its own independent "brand," called World Wide Wrestling Federation. In 1979, that name was shortened to World Wrestling Federation. And finally, in 2002, the name was changed yet again, to World Wrestling Entertainment (WWE). In the course of the biographical profiles, I've chosen wherever possible to give the name of the organization that was in use at the given time. For example, when Antonino Rocca was headlining, it was just Capitol Wrestling; when Bruno Sammartino won the Heavyweight title, it was WWWF; during much of Bob Backlund's reign, it was World Wrestling Federation. When discussing the company and its history as a whole, I use the current name, WWE.

So now let's take a closer look at those giants of the ring who thrived and prospered in WWE's early days. Most of them never had the chance to perform on the mainstream, worldwide stage enjoyed by today's Superstars. Yet they were legends nonetheless, gods to the thousands and thousands of fans who had the honor and privilege of watching them work. Their greatest achievements took place before there were national broadcasts, or the Internet, or merchandise galore. Yet without them, there would not be any of those things today. These are the people who started it all.

WWE LEGENDS

- Vince J. McMahon's final night at Madison Square Garden was the night Hulk Hogan won the Heavyweight title in 1984.

- McMahon is responsible for naming Hogan, Andre the Giant, the Fabulous Moolah, and Haystacks Calhoun.

- Vince Sr. was known for jingling change in his pocket whenever he was concentrating.

The entity known today as World Wrestling Entertainment was previously known as the World Wrestling Federation. Before that, it was the World *Wide* Wrestling Federation. And it started with the company called the Capitol Wrestling Corporation. At the beginning of it all stands one man: Vincent J. McMahon, the founder of WWE. It was this McMahon who, from the 1950s through the '80s, created the most successful wrestling territory of his era, building the foundation upon which his son would one day construct a worldwide empire the likes of which the sport had never before seen.

The elder Vincent McMahon was not the first of the family in the promotional business. Rather, he was introduced to it by his own father, Jess McMahon.

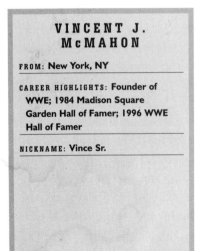

VINCENT J. McMAHON

FROM: New York, NY

CAREER HIGHLIGHTS: Founder of WWE; 1984 Madison Square Garden Hall of Famer; 1996 WWE Hall of Famer

NICKNAME: Vince Sr.

Roderick James "Jess" McMahon was born in New York City in 1880, the son of Irish immigrants who had come to the United States the previous decade. His father had worked hard to establish the family in their new homeland, saving enough money to open up his own tavern and to put Jess through college, a first for the family. However, he could not have predicted what Jess would choose to do with his education after he graduated from Manhattan College in 1902.

Jess McMahon had long been interested in the promotional business. By the time he got out of school, he knew full well what he wanted to be: a promoter. But that became a source of serious family strife.

"Once he went into the promotions business, which was full of charlatans, his father disowned him," recounts WWE chairman Vincent K. McMahon, Jess's grandson. "Because here he had scraped and put his son through college, and was so proud he graduated, but when Jess took his college degree and went into the promotion business—especially, in those days, boxing—his father thought, 'Oh my God, how could you get involved in that sleazy business?' Jess was disowned. And his old man kept to his word. When he died, every nickel he had went to Jess's sister Lottie."

Jess first began making his mark as a promoter in 1911, when he formed the Lincoln Giants, a black baseball team that predated the Negro Leagues by more than a decade. Based out of the Olympic Park ballfield in Harlem, it became one of the most successful ball clubs of its kind. It was also around this time that Jess met his wife, Rose.

On July 6, 1915, Vincent James McMahon was born to Jess and Rose in Harlem, New York. It was just at that time that Jess was really breaking into the business of boxing promotion, which would encompass most of his career. He formed a partnership with Jack Curley, a major New York boxing and wrestling impresario, and the two men put together the historic heavyweight boxing match between champion Jack Johnson and "Great White Hope" Jess Willard in Havana, Cuba.

Young Vincent and his family soon moved from Harlem to the

quiet Far Rockaway section of Queens. For a while, Jess was the matchmaker for the Commonwealth Sporting Club in the Bronx, until 1925 when he was invited by Tex Rickard, then the nation's top boxing promoter, to be the exclusive matchmaker for the new Madison Square Garden Rickard had built on Eighth Avenue and Fifty-ninth Street in Manhattan. Rickard and McMahon presented the first boxing match ever held in the building, a light-heavyweight championship fight between Paul Berlenbach and Jack Delaney.

Despite Jess's burgeoning business, he remained a family man at heart, running a strictly nine-to-five business that assured him time with Rose and Vince. He was known throughout the business as a "debonair, handsome gentleman" whose impeccable neatness earned him the nickname "Dapper Jim." He was also a respectable boxing promoter (which was a rare commodity), even standing up on a number of occasions to the mob, which controlled much of the fight game.

Vincent, meanwhile, was gaining a unique first glimpse of his dad's business. As a child of eleven and twelve, he was regularly brought backstage at Madison Square Garden, and got to know some of the greatest sports heroes of the age. For three years, Jess worked as matchmaker for Tex Rickard at the Garden, until he went into business for himself in 1928, leasing out the New York Coliseum in the Bronx for ten years.

Meanwhile, in Far Rockaway, Vincent enjoyed a middle-class upbringing even as the nation fell into economic depression. He was an avid swimmer in school, and later worked as a lifeguard at Rockaway Beach.

In the early 1930s, with Vincent coming of age, the McMahon family entered the wrestling business for the first time when Jess went back to work for Jack Curley. Boxing was in a lull, and both men turned their full efforts to the grappling game instead. For much of the 1930s and well into the '40s, Jess promoted shows on Long Island for Curley, and later men like Rudy Dusek and Joseph "Toots" Mondt, who controlled most of the wrestling in the New York area.

Vince J. McMahon was brought into the promotional business by his father, who set him up in a small booking office in Hempstead, Long Island, in 1935, promoting fights and concerts. Although Vince was only twenty, he had gained valuable experience assisting his father for years. He worked there for nearly seven years, until the United States was drawn into World War II.

Former heavyweight boxing champion Jack Dempsey, a friend of Vince's, was working as a recruiter for the Coast Guard, and he helped get Vince stationed at the Coast Guard base in Wilmington, North Carolina, where he served throughout the war. There he met a waitress, Vicki, whom he eventually married. They would have two sons, Vincent Kennedy in 1945 and Rod in 1947.

The marriage was an ill-fated one. They split up permanently shortly after Rod's birth, with Vicki remaining in North Carolina and raising the two boys with her new husband. Vince relocated to Washington, D.C., where soon thereafter he met his second wife, Juanita.

Part of Vince's reason for moving to D.C. after the war was to set up his own full-scale wrestling promotion. New York was still under the control of the old-guard promoters like Mondt, and McMahon hoped to use Washington as a foothold to eventually expand throughout the Northeast—most importantly, into the Big Apple. In late 1952, he bought Turner's Arena from Florence Turner, the widow of local promoter Joe Turner, and renamed it the Capitol Arena.

McMahon formed a company he called the Capitol Wrestling Corporation, and presented his first regular wrestling show under the Capitol banner on January 7, 1953. He set up his offices on the seventh floor of Washington's Franklin Park Hotel. At the time, he was using performers on his cards obtained from both Toots Mondt's booking office and the Carolinas office of Jim Crockett Sr. But things would soon change dramatically.

In 1954, McMahon would finally get reacquainted with the two sons he had never really known.

"That came about because my stepmother, Juanita, wanted it to," says Vince McMahon. "She was very interested in the two children that he had fathered. So she came down to North Carolina with my grandmother Rose. I was living with my grandmother on my mom's side at the time. She met me and my brother, Rod, and then subsequently invited us to New York, which is not where my dad was living. They were living in D.C. at the time. But we went to New York first, and visited Rose and Jess, and Juanita and my dad came up and visited. I guess in those days it was easier for my mom's side of the family to accept that we were going to visit our grandparents."

But it would be much more than a visit, as young Vince Kennedy and Rod would be raised for the most part by Vince and Juanita from that point on.

"I loved him from the moment I met him," remembers Vince McMahon of his father. "Just a wonderful, wonderful man."

It was not long after that family reunion that Roderick "Jess" McMahon passed away. At the age of seventy-four, he was still promoting occasional shows, and while in Wilkes-Barre, Pennsylvania, to oversee an event, he died in his sleep on November 22, 1954.

Ironically, it was shortly after Jess's passing that his son's career would begin a meteoric rise that eventually saw him become the preeminent wrestling impresario in the Northeast, and the most successful one in the entire country. From the start, he knew the key to doing this was the brand-new technology that had been working wonders for a handful of promoters in other parts of the nation: television.

"Without question," says his son, Vince K. McMahon, "television was everything."

McMahon began making connections in the TV business, and wired the ramshackle Capitol Arena for TV. In 1955 the Dumont Network (then one of the nation's top TV conglomerates, along with ABC, NBC, and CBS) canceled *Live from the Marigold Theater*, the landmark show out of Chicago that had ushered in a golden age for the wrestling business starting in the late 1940s. Ratings had slumped, and Dumont execs spent much of the next year looking for a full-time replacement.

McMahon convinced the local D.C. Dumont affiliate WTTG to air his weekly matches from the Capitol Arena. On January 5, 1956, the first McMahon-produced wrestling TV program hit the airwaves. The show was an immediate hit with D.C. viewers, and by the summer of 1956, the decision was made to bring Capitol Wrestling to other Dumont affiliates, most importantly WWOR in New York (which still exists to this day as a UPN affiliate, carrying *SmackDown!*).

Capitol Wrestling aired in New York for the first time on June 21, 1956. The success of the show, which featured the white-hot Antonino Rocca as its main attraction, gave McMahon the foothold he needed in the New York market. All he needed now was a way to get past Toots Mondt, the man who controlled all wrestling at Madison Square Garden. The perfect opening occurred when Mondt's promoter's license was suspended for six months by the New York State Athletic Commission (apparently his longtime archenemy Jack Pfefer used his clout with the athletic commission to make Mondt's life difficult).

On November 26, 1956, McMahon held his first event at Madison Square Garden. Wrestling in New York had been in a long slump at that time, and so the Garden was only half full that night. But after word of mouth spread about the colorful, wild and woolly style of wrestling now being presented, the next McMahon engagement drew over 19,000 fans, the largest MSG wrestling crowd in twenty-six years. Vincent J. McMahon was officially a force to be reckoned with.

What followed over the course of the late 1950s was a chaotic promotional war for control of the Northeast. McMahon fought to maintain his foothold in the Garden against the likes of old-guard promoters like Mondt (who still controlled the Manhattan Booking Office, which hired out all the talent) and Pfefer. In addition to D.C. and Manhattan, McMahon would gain sway in places like Baltimore, Philadelphia, Bridgeport, and his home county of Queens. He would also start broadcasting weekly TV shows from the latter two locations as well.

His main advantage was his understanding of television, which many older promoters didn't fully trust. He created revenue by selling advertising for his own programs, and even extended his influence to movie audiences by filming clips of his bouts to air during theater newsreels. By the end of 1960, the war for dominance, for all intents and purposes, was over. When the smoke cleared, out of the more than twenty promoters who had been vying for a piece of the pie, only McMahon remained.

Toots Mondt, out of necessity, at last succumbed to the old adage, "If you can't beat 'em, join 'em." He went into business with Vince as a full partner. It was a perfect teaming: Mondt had the wrestlers, and McMahon had the TV. But from the start, it was clear that McMahon was in charge. He divided promotional rights over the cities he controlled among several business associates such as Mondt, Willie Gilzenberg, Phil Zacko, Ray Fabiani, and others, but maintained power over all of them as chief booking agent for the entire Northeast. Most importantly to him, Madison Square Garden, the arena he had revered since childhood, was now his.

Expansion continued as McMahon next moved into Boston, the last holdout in the region. They had consolidated the largest territory in the country. The next step was to assert their independence and disassociate themselves from the National Wrestling Alliance (NWA), a network of promoters that had outgrown its usefulness. Their ace in the hole was the fact that they had a nearly exclusive agreement with the man who was about to become the next NWA World Champion, Buddy Rogers. McMahon partnered with Chicago promoter Fred Kohler to promote the 1961 Comiskey Park match in which Rogers achieved that goal.

"I remember being there for that as a kid," says Vince McMahon. "That was pretty cool."

Looking to protect the territory he had worked so hard to build, McMahon made the decision to form his own independent organization, under the auspices of the Capitol Wrestling Corporation, which he would ambitiously call World Wide Wrestling Federation (WWWF). In an attempt to block this move, the heads of the NWA brought in Lou Thesz to dethrone Buddy Rogers as champion, but it was no matter to Vince. Using the excuse that the match had been contested under One-Fall rules (back when most title matches were Two-Out-of-Three)—

McMahon and Mondt officially withdrew from the NWA, and recognized Rogers as the first Heavyweight Champion of WWWF in early 1963.

It wasn't clear if WWWF could survive on its own, but once Bruno Sammartino captured the crown, the answer was obvious. With Sammartino as the star, McMahon's organization became the most successful independent territory ever seen. Over the course of the 1960s, McMahon became the most powerful man in the industry. He became a man of means, eventually buying a summer home in Rehoboth Beach, Delaware, and a winter home in Coral Springs, Florida. His almost monthly events at the Garden were followed by lavish parties at Jimmy Weston's Supper Club, a top New York hot spot at the time.

Toots Mondt retired in 1969, selling his stock in the company back to McMahon, who divvied it out to loyal wrestlers Arnold Skaaland and Gorilla Monsoon, as well as longtime associate Phil Zacko. Shortly thereafter, he hired his son Vince as an announcer, also allowing him to get his feet wet as a promoter in Maine, on the northern outskirts of his territory.

Despite a temporary loss of TV coverage at the end of the 1960s, McMahon's fortunes bounced back in the 1970s. The weekly shows moved from Washington, first to Philadelphia, and then to Hamburg and Allentown, Pennsylvania, where they would remain for the rest of his tenure. Madison Square Garden remained his "home field," even when it was closed down in 1968 and a new version was constructed over Penn Station on Seventh Avenue.

"I was just about the last person in the place," recalled Vince Sr. in a rare interview given that year to *Wrestling World* magazine. "All the front doors were locked and I had to leave by way of the employee's entrance. I just sat around thinking back. It felt eerie, thinking about the things that I saw there in the forty-two years since my dad opened it."

In addition to Bruno, over the years McMahon built up top attractions like Andre the Giant, Superstar Billy Graham, Bob Backlund, and Jimmy Snuka. Although his territory remained the Northeast, he would regularly loan out performers like Bruno and

Vince J. McMahon (right) with fellow promoter Frank Tunney.

Andre to other promoters throughout the country and around the world. His territory, particularly the Garden, was the place where every performer in the business wanted to work. Perhaps McMahon's most high-profile venture occurred in 1976, when he co-promoted a match pitting Muhammad Ali against Japanese wrestling star Antonio Inoki that was carried around the globe on closed circuit.

By 1982, McMahon had decided it was time to get out.

"He had just had enough of the business," explains his son Vince. "He had accomplished everything he had ever wanted to accomplish in life. He lived like a king, and that was all he needed.

The business became aggravating. You see, sometimes when performers' personalities mature, they get a different mind-set. To quote my dad, 'They get the wrinkles out of their belly.' Which is an old expression meaning they become less hungry. It required a different set of motivational skills to work with them. My dad was just sick of that kind of shit, dealing with talent that would become ungrateful. You can't blame the talent, it's human nature for you to think, 'I did this,' as opposed to being brutally honest, and saying, 'I did this with the help of all these people.' Dad just lost his zest for the tough part of the business."

The original plan was for the successor to be Gorilla Monsoon (Robert Marella), but Vince K. McMahon, who had developed as a businessman and entrepreneur over the dozen years he had been working for Capitol Wrestling Corporation, offered to buy out his father and all his partners, including Monsoon. In the spring of 1982 Vince Sr., along with partners, met with Vince K. in New York and agreed to sell the company in monthly installments. If the younger McMahon missed a single monthly payment, control would revert back to Vince and his partners.

"It wound up with my dad working for me," says Vincent K. "He threatened to quit on two occasions. And I wouldn't have blamed him if he did, because he didn't know what my intentions were when I bought the business. Because in my view, what was working in the Northeast would work all over the country, and all over the globe. He didn't know I was gonna go in competition with all the cronies he had done business with, his friends. His first and foremost concern was for my longevity; he thought they were gonna kill me. There were a number of threats. But when he threatened to quit the second time, I said, 'Pop, please don't ever do that again. Because the next time you say "That's it, Vinny, I'm gonna quit," I'm gonna have to say okay. I can't do business with you when you're threatening to quit all the time. It's not the right thing to do. When I worked for you, I didn't agree with everything you said, but I did it. Now it's the other way around. It would break my heart if you quit on me.' He finally came full circle. About a month later, he came back to me, and said, 'You know what? You're right.

Fuck all those guys.' That made me feel so good. He could see the success we were having."

As McMahon watched his son begin putting into action his plan to go national with World Wrestling Federation ("Wide" was dropped in 1979), he began experiencing health problems that he tried to keep to himself as long as he could. Eventually, this became impossible, and his friends and family convinced him to see a doctor in early 1984. What was originally diagnosed as a minor prostate ailment turned out to be pancreatic cancer.

"In those days, I don't know that they could have done anything about it, even if it had been properly diagnosed at first," says Vince McMahon. "By the time they discovered he was really sick, they gave him chemo and his hair fell out. He was always so proud of his hair. He had a hell of a head of hair."

Recalling his dad's last days in a 2000 *Playboy* interview, Vince said, "My dad was old Irish, and for some reason I don't understand, they don't show affection. He never told me he loved me. That time in the hospital, I kissed him and said I loved him. He didn't like to be kissed, but I took advantage of him. Then I started to go. I hadn't quite gotten through the door when I heard him yell, 'I love you, Vinny!'"

After a four-month hospital battle, Vincent James McMahon passed away on May 27, 1984, at age sixty-eight. He was survived by Juanita, Vince, and Rod, as well as his two grandchildren, fourteen-year-old Shane and seven-year-old Stephanie. Ironically, just as had been the case with his own father, Jess, Vincent himself died just before his son would achieve his greatest success. In the years immediately following, the World Wrestling Federation, under Vincent K. McMahon's Titan Sports, would ignite a new golden age for the sport, conquer the wrestling business, and become one of the most well known entertainment companies on the planet.

The product that Vince Sr. created would eventually come to be known as World Wrestling Entertainment. And although today's multimedia sports entertainment giant is far removed from those old Capitol Wrestling days in so many ways, Vincent J. McMahon remains the man who started it all.

- Some of the stars Mondt helped create from the 1920s through the 1960s included Wayne "Big" Munn, Jim Londos, Antonino Rocca, Bruno Sammartino, and Cowboy Bill Watts.

- Toots was known for his willingness to eat virtually anything, no matter how disgusting!

He was an ingenious innovator, and a feared enforcer. A brilliant businessman, and a degenerate gambler. He forever changed the very concept of pro wrestling, and his often-cutthroat practices led his enemies to remember him as "corrupt to his soul." He would help to create the most powerful dynasty the sport had ever seen, only to watch it collapse around him; then go on to become the most powerful promoter in the country, only to be forced out by a virtually unknown newcomer, who would later become his closest ally and benefactor.

There are few figures in wrestling history more enigmatic than Joe "Toots" Mondt, who in his early years virtually reinvented the sport, and in his latter years helped create an empire that continues to dominate the industry to this day.

Joseph Raymond Mondt was born on an Iowa farm in 1894.

TOOTS MONDT

FROM: Greeley, CO

YEARS IN WWE: 1960–76

CAREER HIGHLIGHTS: Creator of modern pro wrestling format; cofounder of World Wide Wrestling Federation

When the farm went bankrupt, the Mondt family moved to Greeley, Colorado, where Joe's father worked in the mines. In tremendous shape thanks to a childhood of farm work, Joe further perfected his body by turning to the art of wrestling, a sport then taking the nation by storm for the first time.

He subscribed to the wrestling correspondence course of Martin "Farmer" Burns, the legendary trainer of Frank Gotch and many other early greats. In 1910, pro wrestling was still a thriving carnival attraction, and that was where the sixteen-year-old Mondt made his debut, challenging the wrestler who was part of a traveling show passing through Greeley. As it turned out, the youngster was far from the easy "marks" the carnies had grown used to fleecing of their money. He had true grappling skill, and in fact had learned the skills of "hooking"—the application of potentially crippling holds—from the Farmer Burns course.

Before long, Mondt found himself on the other side of the situation, traveling with the carnivals as a regular employee, taking on hapless locals in town after town. It was while touring that Mondt was discovered by the very man who had indirectly led him to the business, Farmer Burns.

Mondt became part of Burns's training camp and started competing in arenas against other professional wrestlers for the first time. The Farmer would be responsible for the nickname that would stick with him for the rest of his life, even long after it was accurate. Taking one look at the youngster's boyish appearance, Burns christened him "Toots."

Toots's wrestling career was not where he achieved his greatness. It was behind the scenes that he quickly began building a reputation. Still in his twenties, he was considered highly valuable as a trainer and sparring partner, and his instinctive business sense was already getting him attention.

In 1919, the course of wrestling history was altered when Toots Mondt crossed paths with Billy Sandow, a paranoid and often difficult promoter, and the man he represented, a tough-as-nails grappler from Nekoosa, Wisconsin, named Robert Friedrich, better known as Ed "Strangler" Lewis. He was introduced to them by

Burns, and became a valuable asset immediately. Together, the three men would gain control of the entire business, and come to be known as the Gold Dust Trio.

It started in part from Mondt's desire to remake the sport into something it had never been before. Up to that point, matches normally went on for hours and consisted of very little movement or action, with opponents engaging in subtle wrestling techniques that often bored crowds. Furthermore, matches were made in haphazard fashion, with very little buildup. After convincing Lewis and Sandow, Toots would change all this.

He introduced what he called "Slam Bang Western Wrestling," a style that incorporated striking, kicking, and other types of blows—in other words, maneuvers that were not really "holds" in the true sense. This created more action and excitement. He instituted time limits, which caused wrestlers to speed up their matches. Entertaining the crowd became a top priority. In order to properly hype the matches presented by the Gold Dust Trio, Mondt created the concept of the "program," an ongoing feud that would generate interest and help build up new stars. For the first time, competitors were divided into clearly defined "good guys" and "bad guys." This was made even easier by the Trio's idea of presenting wrestling for the first time as a "packaged" touring attraction, with an established troupe of competitors appearing together in each city. The sport has remained more or less in the same form ever since.

The Gold Dust Trio's dominance was also helped along by Lewis's status as World Champion, a distinction he would hold throughout much of the 1920s. With the Strangler as the top draw, the Trio established a central booking office for the entire industry. They presented their own shows, but in addition, any promoter anywhere who wished to use their performers had to go through them to do it. Not until the national expansion of World Wrestling Federation in the 1980s would a single entity gain such sway over the sport.

But it couldn't last forever. By the end of the 1920s, the Gold Dust Trio came apart as infighting and pettiness took root. A series of misguided business decisions by Sandow, as well as Sandow's insistence on bringing his brother Max into the group, led Mondt to walk out. Using his connections in New York and throughout the Northeast, he helped create a new World Championship, under the auspices of the newly formed National Wrestling Association (the original NWA), an extension of the National Boxing Association (which exists today as the World Boxing Association—WBA). The title went to German-born Dick Shikat, but it was the man Shikat lost it to, Jim Londos, who would become a legitimate rival to Strangler Lewis.

Mondt went to work for Jack Curley, the man who then controlled the New York wrestling scene. When Curley passed away in 1937, Mondt got the opportunity he had been craving all along. He usurped complete control of the New York operation from the Curley organization—pushing out Curley's sons in the process—and set himself up as the Big Apple's wrestling kingpin.

The 1930s and '40s would see a string of relentless promotional wars, with alliances changing on a regular basis and treachery everywhere. But by the end of the 1940s, it was over. Toots had established himself as the uncontested overlord of wrestling in the northeastern United States, running his Manhattan Booking Office out of the Holland Hotel on Forty-second Street.

The tactics he employed to achieve this end were often unsavory, to say the least. Mondt was ruthless, and the legends that sprung up around him are numerous. He was accused by some of skimming from wrestlers' payoffs. He wasn't afraid to use his very real and very dangerous physical abilities, and it's believed that he would occasionally rough up those who didn't see things his way. His victims reportedly included Shikat, as well as Londos, whom he roughed up in the lobby of New York's Astor Hotel when the World Champion refused to do business with him. His gambling addiction was Mondt's downfall, and much of the fortune he amassed would be spent at the racetrack. His business was driven to a large degree by the need to pay off his debts, and it's believed that he once sold off his wife's wardrobe for this purpose.

In the 1950s, Mondt's hold on the Northeast was challenged by a Washington, D.C., promoter named Vincent James McMahon. Through his connections in the television industry, as well as his wooing of Mondt's top attraction Antonino Rocca, McMahon gained a foothold in the region, even running shows in Mondt's main stronghold, Madison Square Garden. After battling on and off for years, the tide would turn decidedly in McMahon's favor, and by 1960 Mondt had to face reality: He had been replaced. But the new regime would not spell the end of his promotional career. Recognizing his value, the victorious McMahon made the ousted Mondt his full partner.

"See, my dad was not a wrestler," explains WWE chairman Vincent K. McMahon. "He needed someone who understood the ins and outs of the business. Toots could be a badass, and my dad had him as a partner, because if you had a problem in those days and you needed someone to straighten it out, Toots would be the guy to straighten it out. Or at least that was the perception. He was a big, barrel-chested, tough son of a bitch. And looked the part too, with great big old nasty cauliflower ears. But really a sweetheart of a man."

With Mondt as his ally, McMahon would break away from the National Wrestling Alliance and create his own independent entity—World Wide Wrestling Federation—in 1963. The McMahon/Mondt organization would control the entire Northeast, Toots's longtime domain, and become the most lucrative operation in the business. And Mondt was there through all those formative years, using his connections and accumulated wisdom to help McMahon build his empire. He even took up permanent residence in the Franklin Park Hotel in D.C., WWWF's base of operations.

By 1969, a combination of health and financial problems were finally getting to the old warhorse. His weight had ballooned to over 300 pounds, and at age seventy-five, this was taking its toll on his legs and ankles. His penchant for the ponies had ruined him, and he was forced to go into hock. Eager to get off the road, he retired, selling his 50 percent of the company back to McMahon. He moved to St. Louis, where he was cared for by his niece as excessive weight and old age caused his health to deteriorate ever further. On June 11, 1976, Mondt died at age eighty-two. Until that day, he had remained on the payroll of Vince J. McMahon, who made sure always to take care of his longtime partner and confidant.

- Famed maestro Arturo Toscanini, a rabid wrestling fan, was good friends with Rocca.

- Rocca was depicted wrestling Superman on the cover of an August 1962 comic book.

- The 1976 horror film *Alice, Sweet Alice*, featuring child actress Brooke Shields, includes Rocca in a bit part.

In the 1950s, there was no bigger wrestling star on the East Coast than Antonino Rocca. With the exception of Gorgeous George, he was the greatest box-office attraction of his era. During the infancy of Capitol Wrestling, the company that would become WWE, Rocca was the key to the success of upstart promoter Vincent J. McMahon. For the first decade of Capitol's existence, he was the undisputed king of the ring. His amazing acrobatic feats made him the forerunner to innovative performers like Mil Mascaras, Jimmy "Superfly" Snuka, and Rey Mysterio.

Rocca was born Antonio Biasetton in 1923—along with a twin sister—in the Italian town of Treviso, near Venice. At fifteen, with the threat of war looming in his Fascist-controlled homeland,

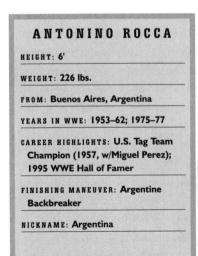

ANTONINO ROCCA

HEIGHT: 6'

WEIGHT: 226 lbs.

FROM: Buenos Aires, Argentina

YEARS IN WWE: 1953–62; 1975–77

CAREER HIGHLIGHTS: U.S. Tag Team Champion (1957, w/Miguel Perez); 1995 WWE Hall of Famer

FINISHING MANEUVER: Argentine Backbreaker

NICKNAME: Argentina

he and his family immigrated to the city of Rosario in the South American nation of Argentina, a popular destination for expatriate Italians.

During his lifetime, Rocca had a penchant for outrageous exaggeration and outright fabrication, so what is known of his pre-wrestling career is shrouded in doubt. What's for certain is that he was a remarkable athlete, excelling in rugby and soccer. He nearly became a successful soccer player in Argentina, but a knee injury ended that.

In 1947 Biasetton began wrestling professionally in Argentina, where Stanislaus Zbysko, a famous World Champion wrestler of the early twentieth century, was running the local promotion. Biasetton changed his name to Rocca, playing up his Italian heritage, and adapted the incredible flexibility and agility he had used on the soccer field to the wrestling ring. Former American wrestler Nick Elitch spotted the high-flying Rocca while vacationing in Argentina in 1948.

Elitch convinced the twenty-five-year-old, who barely spoke any English, to make him his manager and come with him to the United States. In June 1948 he arrived on American soil and went to work for Houston promoter Morris Sigel, an associate of Elitch. He had his first matches in Galveston and Houston, where he defeated Lord James Blears.

An immediate success, Rocca wowed fans who had never seen an athlete of his type in a wrestling ring. In an era when wrestlers never left the mat and often clinched in holds for minutes at a time, Rocca brought a new, fast-paced excitement. He couldn't wrestle very much—and this often made him unpopular with his peers—but his flashy repertoire of aerial maneuvers like dropkicks, hurracanranas, and victory rolls dazzled spectators and made up for any lack of grappling technique. This was unprecedented, and literally changed what pro wrestling was for the generations that have followed.

Before long, other promoters were requesting Rocca, and Sigel began lending him out. In 1949, while competing in St. Louis, he was approached by veteran wrestler Kola Kwariani. The grizzled Russian convinced Rocca that New York was where the real money was, and stole him away from Elitch and the entire Houston contingent.

Kwariani became Rocca's manager and brought him to the Big Apple to work for Joseph "Toots" Mondt, a longtime promoter who was struggling to resurrect the wrestling business in the New York area. With a unique performer like Rocca, Mondt knew he could finally accomplish that.

Rocca agreed to an exclusive deal with Mondt's Manhattan Booking Office and took a three-room apartment on West Fifty-seventh Street. He made his area debut in Brooklyn at the Ridgewood Grove with a victory over Benito Gardini. On December 12, 1949, Mondt brought Rocca to Madison Square Garden, where he defeated "Mr. America" Gene Stanlee. A crowd of 17,854 witnessed the match, the largest Garden crowd in eighteen years. Just like that, wrestling in New York was back in business.

"He was the star of the Manhattan Booking Office," remembers longtime referee and wrestler Dick Kroll. "A very nice guy, very flamboyant, given to great exaggeration. He would claim he'd never been defeated; he would claim that he killed a man in South America. He was a braggart, but a fun braggart to be around."

In addition to his groundbreaking wrestling style, it was Rocca's ethnicity that brought in the masses. An Italian from Latin America, he had tremendous drawing power among both populations in the New York area. Not only did he become the greatest New York attraction since 1930s World Champion Jim Londos, but his agent, Toots Mondt, began booking him for promoters all over the country—and raking in a hefty chunk of the profits. Inspired by his client's limber acrobatics, Mondt once remarked, "Rocca has done more for legs than Betty Grable."

Lesser promoters throughout the Northeast area were given access to Rocca on a regular basis. One of these was Vincent J. McMahon, whose Capitol Wrestling Corporation had begun presenting matches in Washington, D.C., at the start of 1953. Rocca was a fixture on the earliest McMahon cards, and helped the fledgling promoter carve out a successful territory for himself.

"Who could forget him?" asks WWE chairman Vincent K.

McMahon. "In the old Madison Square Garden, I used to see Rocca perform. Oh my God, what an unbelievably charismatic and athletic performer. The stuff he could do was incredible. All kinds of aerial stuff."

When Vincent J. McMahon secured a national television deal with the Dumont Network in the summer of 1956, he persuaded Rocca to leave Mondt and work for him. An old-school promoter, Mondt had never had much faith in TV, which proved his downfall. Rocca became McMahon's attraction, and by the fall of 1956 Capitol's stock had raised to such a degree that McMahon had the leverage to move Mondt out of the Garden.

On November 26, the first McMahon-promoted event was held at the Garden, and featured Rocca beating Dick the Bruiser. Over the course of the late 1950s, McMahon's power in the Northeast grew, and Rocca became a bigger star than ever. He bought a $6 million textile mill in Argentina and was given his own daily radio show. Eventually McMahon and Mondt set aside their differences and, with Rocca as their top star, joined forces to become the most powerful promotional force wrestling had seen since the Gold Dust Trio of the 1920s (of which Mondt had been one).

"I used to tag team with Rocca," says veteran WWE wrestler and manager Arnold Skaaland. "He was a great guy. Good talker. He liked to b.s. a lot. I'd say, 'Rocca, where you been?' And he'd say, 'Arnie, you wouldn't believe it, but these Navy pilots took me over Cuba!' He'd come up with a lot of stuff like that. But he had a good heart."

"He was a great bullshitter," adds Vince McMahon. "But half his stories were true, and you didn't know what to believe. 'I'm working for the CIA down in Ecuador. . . .' I think that was true. He would go on these missions and shit. What was fact, what was fiction? You never knew with Tony."

In 1957 Rocca entered a new chapter of his career, forming a legendary partnership with Puerto Rican Superstar Miguel Perez. They would be a regular Tag Team for the next four years. In March 1957, they defeated Jackie Fargo & Don Stevens to become the first holders of Capitol's first title—the U.S. Tag Team Championship. Their feud with Dr. Jerry Graham & Eddie Graham would go down in

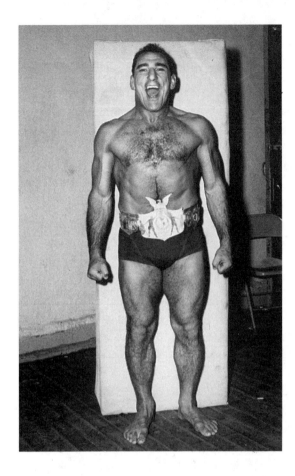

wrestling history. From 1958 to 1960, Rocca & Perez headlined the Garden against the Graham Brothers on seven different occasions.

By 1960, Capitol Sports had become the uncontested ruler of wrestling in the Northeast. But it was just about that time that Rocca's star began to wane. Buddy Rogers was overtaking him as the company's top draw, and a new ethnic hero, Bruno Sammartino, was swiftly gaining steam. By the end of 1962, with McMahon and Mondt planning on breaking away from the NWA, starting World Wide Wrestling Federation and making Sammartino their top star, Rocca walked out on the promotion in bitterness.

Feeling vindictive toward his former employers, Rocca allied himself with Mid-Atlantic promoter Jim Crockett Sr., a leading member of the NWA—whose members also had an axe to grind.

With the Argentine as its top star, Crockett Promotions attempted an invasion of McMahon territory in the mid-1960s, running shows in places like Long Island, Brooklyn, and New Jersey. They even got television coverage, but it was still a resounding failure.

Rocca had not managed his money very well during his heyday—preferring to live the high life—and was now feeling the effects. Not only his financial status suffered, but his health as well, as years of heavy boozing took their toll.

"The poor bastard only got a third of every nickel he ever made," recalls Vince McMahon. "A tremendous draw, but he didn't get what was due him financially. He had his demons as well. Tony was the kind of guy, when you're having a good time, he was the greatest guy in the world to be around, but when you were having a bad time, you didn't want to be around him."

Rocca continued competing in obscurity into the 1970s, and in 1975, an amazing thing happened. Choosing to let bygones be bygones, McMahon, now the sole kingpin of WWWF, hired Antonino as a television announcer. Recognizing he still had appeal to the area's Italian and Latino populations, Vince Sr. paired him up with his son, future WWE chairman Vincent K. McMahon, as a regular broadcast team.

In early 1977 Rocca took time off from announcing to briefly come out of retirement in Puerto Rico. He returned to the States with an acute case of food poisoning that, coupled with his already weakened constitution, caused his kidneys to fail. He passed away on March 16. Although he was either fifty-three or fifty-four at the time, embellishments surrounded Rocca in death as in life, and it was publicly stated that he was only forty-nine.

One of the most successful performers to ever work for the McMahons, Rocca is often overlooked because his glory years occurred before the creation of the WWWF name. Yet to disregard him in any rundown of the company's top Superstars would be doing a tremendous disservice to wrestling history. Antonino Rocca was one of those rare performers who combine box-office appeal with genuine innovation, leaving the sport different from the way they found it.

- Rogers is credited with developing both the figure-four leglock and the atomic drop.

- Comedian Andy Kaufman idolized Rogers as a child and brought him on *Saturday Night Live* with him in 1979.

- A mural of the record Comiskey Park crowd from the night he won the NWA World title hung on a wall in Rogers's home.

Innovator. Pioneer. Top box-office draw. Buddy Rogers was all these things, and then some. He created a persona and performing style that would influence countless wrestlers who followed him. A figure of major historical importance, he stood at the center of the controversy that led to the creation of World Wide Wrestling Federation. In fact, he was the first holder of the WWWF Heavyweight title, which still exists today as the WWE Championship.

He was born Herman Rohde on February 20, 1921, in Camden, New Jersey, the son of German immigrants. As many immigrants

BUDDY ROGERS

HEIGHT: 6'

WEIGHT: 235 lbs.

FROM: Camden, NJ

YEARS IN WWE: 1960–63; 1982–83

CAREER HIGHLIGHTS: NWA United States Champion (1950–61); NWA World Champion (1961–63); WWWF Heavyweight Champion (1963); 2-time U.S. Tag Team Champion (1960, w/Johnny Valentine; 1962–63, w/Johnny Barend); 1994 WWE Hall of Famer

FINISHING MANEUVER: Figure-four leglock

NICKNAMES: The Nature Boy; Dutch

and sons of immigrants did in those days, he joined the police force shortly after turning eighteen.

That same year, 1939, Rohde began wrestling professionally on a local basis. At first, he used his birth name, but soon became known in the ring as Dutch Rogers. Although the "Rogers" part downplayed his ethnicity, "Dutch" came from a nickname he had gotten—and would always retain—due to his German (*Deutsche*) ancestry.

The 1940s was a tough time for the sport. While many of the legitimately skilled grapplers were fighting in the war and business was slumping, promoters were looking for outrageous characters to grab the attention of fans. The man who set the standard was Gorgeous George, who first emerged as the sport's top star in the early 1940s.

But shortly after that, Herman Rohde would take some key elements of what George created and modify them into a persona that would literally change wrestling. While wrestling in Texas in 1944, he changed his name to Buddy Rogers, after a popular B-movie star of the time. Dying his hair platinum, donning sequined ring jackets, and adopting an excessively cocky demeanor, he became an entirely new kind of performer.

"Buddy Rogers was an out-and-out star," wrote the Fabulous Moolah, a former valet of Rogers, in her autobiography. "He had a knack for what we call ring showmanship. No one was better at it than Buddy Rogers. Buddy Rogers . . . owned every moment in the ring. You'd watch him and forget he had an opponent."

The epitome of the wrestling villain, Rogers quickly gained the attention of fans—who detested him for his arrogant strut and cowardly tactics. In an era of extended holds, many of the roughhouse, high-impact maneuvers he used were very innovative for the time and have since become parts of any wrestler's basic repertoire. This, in addition to his mastery of ring psychology, would redefine what it meant to be a professional wrestler, and many competitors would follow suit in the ensuing years and decades. Perhaps chief among these was Ric Flair, a huge Rogers fan who adopted everything from his strut to his hair, his figure-four, and his nickname of Nature Boy.

Buddy Rogers became wrestling's original Nature Boy while competing in California in 1947. In addition to his impeccable physique, Rogers always maintained a golden brown tan, and the California crowds, during an era way before the rise of political correctness, took to chanting "Nature Boy" at him—a reference to a popular song of the day sung by Nat "King" Cole, an African-American.

"Buddy was so flamboyant," remembers Vince McMahon, who admired him greatly as a teenager. "He had a great physique and was very charismatic. Buddy was also very reliable. A tremendous athlete—Buddy was far and away one of the best athletes ever in the business. And very smart, in the ring and outside the ring."

Outside the ring, Rogers also gained a reputation among his peers for being nearly as arrogant and obnoxious as he was inside it. The Fabulous Moolah tells the tale of being kicked out of his car while traveling between towns when she refused to give in to his advances. Once in 1962, he was roughed up in the locker room by Karl Gotch and Dr. Bill Miller, two tough-as-nails grapplers who had a bone to pick with him and sent him fleeing the building in nothing but his jockstrap.

Nevertheless, Rogers was cocky because he could back it up with his sheer ability to draw money like nobody's business. With television bringing wrestling into homes across America for the first time, Buddy Rogers became one of the sport's main attractions. His base of operations in those days was Columbus, Ohio, then a wrestling hotbed promoted by Al Haft. Haft would often lend Rogers out to other National Wrestling Alliance promoters, particularly Sam Muchnick of St. Louis, the territory Rogers almost single-handedly turned into the flagship of the fledgling NWA.

On New Year's Day 1950, Rogers became the first NWA United States Champion, beating Johnny Valentine in a tournament final. Although other versions of the title would pop up in other territories, he would hold the original for eleven years, the longest reign ever for a men's championship of any kind.

His promoter in the Northeast was the eccentric impresario Jack Pfefer, for whom Rogers was the crown jewel of his collection

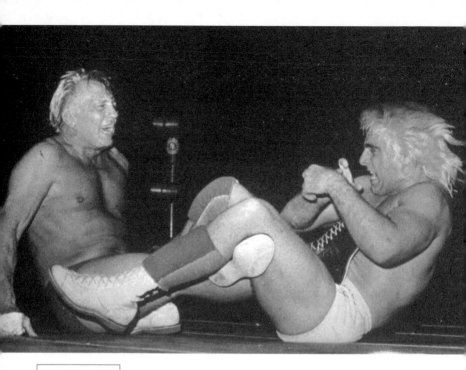

Rogers vs. Flair.

of traveling showmen, oddballs, and freaks. At the time, Pfefer was fighting the growing influence of rival promoters Toots Mondt—his old partner who controlled the Manhattan Booking Office—and Vincent J. McMahon, whose Capitol Wrestling Corporation was gaining more and more leverage in the region.

Once Mondt and McMahon formed their alliance in 1960, they made a move that consolidated their power in the Northeast and pushed Pfefer out of the New York area for good. They then lured Buddy Rogers into their camp.

Meanwhile, Rogers continued to work for other NWA promoters. On June 30, 1961, he faced NWA World Champion Pat O'Connor in Comiskey Park. The bout was witnessed by 38,622 fans, making it the biggest-drawing NWA World title match ever. Buddy Rogers became World Champion that night, and when presented the title belt, grabbed the house mic and uttered in typical fashion, "To a nicer guy, it couldn't happen."

But there was a problem. Rogers was becoming the exclusive talent of McMahon and Mondt, and now that he was World Champion, he was an even more valuable attraction. His bookings were completely controlled by Capitol Wrestling, and it became rare for Rogers to defend the title anywhere but the Northeast. The other NWA promoters raised a fuss, but to no avail. From March 1961 to May 1963, Rogers was the main event in twenty-three out of twenty-six cards put on by Capitol at the Garden, creating the company's most successful period up to that point.

In spite of his drawing power, the NWA bigwigs no longer wanted Rogers as champion if they couldn't use him. Legendary former champion Lou Thesz was brought out of retirement for the purpose of taking the gold. Try as he might, Rogers couldn't get out of defending the title against the renowned grappler, and when he and Thesz finally met in Toronto on January 24, 1963, it marked the end of Rogers's time as NWA World Champion.

This turn of events would bring about Capitol Wrestling's withdrawal from the NWA and the creation of the independent entity called WWWF (known today as WWE). Mondt and McMahon refused to acknowledge Rogers's defeat, in part because it was a One-Fall match instead of the traditional Two-Out-of-Three—although this merely gave them the excuse they needed to declare their much-wanted independence. They planned to recognize Rogers as the first-ever WWWF World Heavyweight Champion, but those plans were momentarily derailed when the Nature Boy suffered a heart attack in March of 1963.

Things got back on track in April, and the WWWF took off with Rogers as its titleholder. The situation didn't last long, however; the Nature Boy was forty-two years old and in questionable health, and there was a hungry challenger in town: twenty-seven-year-old Bruno Sammartino. On May 17, 1963, the two met in Madison Square Garden, and it took only 48 seconds for Bruno to force Buddy into submission with his Italian Backbreaker, starting his eight-year reign as champion.

By the end of the summer, Rogers had retired. He was gone from the scene until 1978, when he made a comeback at the age of fifty-seven. He settled into the Carolinas territory as a manager, handling the careers of, among others, Jimmy "Superfly" Snuka. It was also around this time that Rogers matched up with the young man who had adopted his gimmick, Ric Flair. Shortly after losing a "Battle of the Nature Boys" to Flair, Rogers departed the area.

In 1982 Rogers returned to the World Wrestling Federation, then run by Vincent K. McMahon, the son of his former employer. He was given a weekly interview segment called "Rogers Corner," and once again became Jimmy Snuka's manager, allying with him against Snuka's former manager Capt. Lou Albano.

Rogers left the sport for good at the end of 1983, and retired to Florida shortly thereafter. Although he maintained a strict exercise regimen that helped him keep up his amazing physique into old age, Rogers's heart problems worsened, and he underwent a quadruple bypass in the late 1980s.

In 1992 Rogers nearly came out of retirement at age seventy-one to take on yet another "Nature Boy," Buddy Landell, for Joel Goodhart's Tri-State Wrestling Alliance, the Philadelphia-based forerunner to ECW. Unfortunately, health problems prevented the match from happening. In June, Rogers suffered a series of strokes that left him comatose.

On Friday, July 6, 1992, Herman "Dutch" Rohde passed away in Fort Lauderdale, Florida. The legacy of Buddy Rogers that Rohde left behind is one very few competitors can dream of creating, and persists to this day. Every time Ric Flair styles and profiles, every time Vince McMahon struts arrogantly to the ring, every time Triple H infuriates a crowd with his ·treacherous tactics, the influence of Buddy Rogers is felt. In a sport in which the word *icon* is thrown about so frequently, he was the original.

- Skaaland served as referee for the famous 1962 match between Freddie Blassie and Rikidozan in Japan.
- Skaaland was Vince McMahon Sr.'s partner. His responsibilities included running WWWF shows in Westchester (where he resided) and serving as a handler for Andre the Giant.
- Skaaland can be spotted in the 1987 "Piledriver" video as the foreman of a construction site.

In the pantheon of wrestling managers, there is one man who stands out as sports entertainment's equivalent of Vince Lombardi or Casey Stengel. He is Arnold Skaaland, the guiding force behind both Bruno Sammartino and Bob Backlund, considered by some to be the two greatest WWE Champions of all time. Just having managed one of those men would be enough to place him among the greats, but having managed both may just make him the greatest of all. With the exception of a ten-month period during which the title was held by Superstar Billy Graham, Arnold Skaaland was the manager of the Heavyweight Champion from December 1973 to December 1983.

ARNOLD SKAALAND

HEIGHT: 5'11"

WEIGHT: 205 lbs.

FROM: White Plains, NY

YEARS IN WWE: 1953–present

CAREER HIGHLIGHTS: WWWF U.S. Tag Team Champion (1967, w/Spiros Arion); 1996 WWE Hall of Famer

NICKNAME: The Golden Boy

Because of his stellar managerial career, many forget that Skaaland was a wrestler long before he was a manager. He was born January 21, 1925, in White Plains, New York. As a very young man, he served in the U.S. Marines during World War II. Following his military service, he had a successful turn as an amateur boxer. But amateur boxing wasn't paying the bills, and in 1946 he turned to professional wrestling.

At the time, professional wrestling was embarking on a golden age, thanks to the advent of television. Its popularity was at an all-time high, as viewers across the nation tuned in to the national broadcast from Chicago's Marigold Arena, featuring stars that would soon become household names, including the likes of Buddy Rogers, Johnny Valentine, and Gorgeous George. In the northeastern United States, where Skaaland spent much of his time competing, the promotion that would eventually become World Wide Wrestling Federation was just taking shape in Washington, D.C., with Vincent J. McMahon at the helm. However, the top promoters in the Northeast at the time were Rudy Dusek and Joseph "Toots" Mondt, who ran shows at Madison Square Garden in partnership with Chicago promoter Fred Kohler and several other regional promoters.

Known as the Golden Boy, Skaaland made his first appearance at Madison Square Garden—the stronghold of the Northeast—in January 1952, as part of a card organized as a benefit for the Italian Relief Fund and headlined by Antonino Rocca vs. Primo Carnera. Over the course of the 1950s, as WWWF took over MSG and grew to become the dominant northeastern company, the Golden Boy went along for the ride, becoming one of the fixtures of Federation programming during the 1950s and '60s. Although he was never one of the main attractions as a wrestler, he went home with the winner's share of the purse more often than not. In June 1967, he was chosen by Greek Superstar Spiros Arion to replace his departing partner Antonio Pugliese as half of the U.S. Tag Team Champions. Skaaland & Arion would lose the title the following month to Lou Albano & Tony Altimore—the Sicilians.

As the 1960s rolled to a close, Skaaland called an end to his in-

ring career. But middle age had not brought an end to his activities in the business. Having become a close associate and adviser to Vince J. McMahon, over the years, Skaaland went on to become a business partner, gaining part ownership in the Capitol Wrestling Corporation, the company that then operated WWWF.

"Vince was a hell of a man," remembers Skaaland. "He had me take care of a lot of the shows, because he usually didn't travel. I would go all around New England, pick up the money, pay off the boys, and bring the money back down to Washington [WWWF headquarters]."

But the most notable chapter in his career had already begun in 1963. When Bruno Sammartino became WWWF Heavyweight Champion, Skaaland became his manager. He would remain so for the rest of Bruno's tenure in the company. He represented Sammartino during his monumental first reign from 1963 to 1971, as well as when he regained the title from Stan "The Man" Stasiak in December 1973. Sammartino and Skaaland were inseparable. Decked out in his impeccable suits and sporting his trademark slicked-back hair and spit curl, Skaaland could be seen walking the aisle with the "Living Legend" for each and every one of his matches, even after he lost the gold for the final time in April 1977.

Such a role would have been more than enough of a swan song for Skaaland's amazing thirty-five-year on-air career. But he wasn't finished. In 1977, Skaaland hooked up with a promising young amateur-turned-pro by the name of Bob Backlund. The following year, he guided Backlund to the Heavyweight Championship, and remained with him through his six years on top of the Federation.

"He was a terrific wrestler," Skaaland says. "Strong. Unbelievable how strong he was and how he could wrestle. I traveled all over with him. Same thing with Bruno."

Backlund's loss of the title to the Iron Sheik on December 26, 1983, was a result of the most well known and controversial incident of Skaaland's career. With his protégé trapped in the Sheik's dreaded camel clutch submission hold but refusing to quit, Skaaland threw in the towel, signaling a forfeiture to the referee. It was a difficult decision to make, but Skaaland knew that Backlund was going into the match with an injured neck and risked serious aggravation of that injury with his never-say-die attitude.

The former champion and his manager parted ways after that night, and Skaaland brought his managerial career to a close. World Wrestling Federation was quickly becoming a very different place. With Capitol Wrestling a thing of the past and the Federation under the control of Vincent K. McMahon, the company was spreading out from a regional northeastern promotion to a national phenomenon. It was at that point that Skaaland chose to step into the background.

As a trusted associate of Vince's father, he was granted a position as a backstage agent, which he maintained throughout the remainder of the 1980s and much of the early '90s.

In 1996, "The Golden Boy" Arnold Skaaland was inducted into the World Wrestling Federation Hall of Fame, the ultimate reward for years of loyal service to the company and its fans. At the age of eighty, he's now retired, but nevertheless remains a valued member of the WWE family. He's been known to pop up backstage at WWE events in the New York area with his wife, Betty, visiting old friends who know him simply as "Arnie." He's even been known to lend a hand with various behind-the-scenes activities.

Whether it's been called pro wrestling or sports entertainment, this is the business Arnold Skaaland has known and loved for more than half a century. His days of wrestling and managing may long be over, but his passion continues to drive him to be a part of it all.

- The Captain played video game character Mario in a Saturday-morning *Super Mario Brothers* TV series.

- Albano was a regular guest on the long-running *Joe Franklin* talk show, and is a good friend of Franklin.

- In the video for "Girls Just Want to Have Fun," Albano played Cyndi Lauper's father.

Gorilla Monsoon once called him "the biggest walking advertisement for birth control I've ever seen." And he once summed up his own talents by saying, "I'm a good bullshitter." But don't hold that against Capt. Lou Albano.

The pride of Mount Vernon, New York, Lou Albano was just about as eccentric as they come, a character among characters. His outrageous histrionics brought an element of the vaudevillian to the pro wrestling stage, and at his peak, his were among the most recognizable names and faces in the game. Some label him the best wrestling manager who ever lived, with seventeen World Tag Team Champions to his credit, as well as several other titleholders.

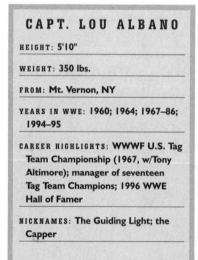

CAPT. LOU ALBANO

HEIGHT: 5'10"

WEIGHT: 350 lbs.

FROM: Mt. Vernon, NY

YEARS IN WWE: 1960; 1964; 1967–86; 1994–95

CAREER HIGHLIGHTS: WWWF U.S. Tag Team Championship (1967, w/Tony Altimore); manager of seventeen Tag Team Champions; 1996 WWE Hall of Famer

NICKNAMES: The Guiding Light; the Capper

Louis Albano was born July 29, 1933, in Rome, Italy, but the family moved to the United States shortly after his birth. His father, Carmen Albano, had been one of Mount Vernon's busiest obstetricians, reportedly delivering upward of five thousand babies into that fair Westchester burg. Three of Lou's brothers entered the field of education, with two of them eventually becoming school principals. By the beginning of the 1950s, Lou himself had made it as far as premed. But his destiny lay along a different path.

"He wasn't dealing with a full deck," explained colleague "Classy" Freddie Blassie in his autobiography, *Listen, You Pencil Neck Geeks.* "There's no question he knew wrestling from A to Z. Switch the subject to anything else, though, and you could see that his mind wasn't functioning right."

Albano abandoned his academic pursuits for military service. Looking to break into professional boxing, he approached promoter Willy Gilzenberg, who handled the careers of such fighters as "Two Ton" Tony Galento and Red Cochrane. However, Gilzenberg deemed Albano too short, and suggested he try wrestling instead. At the time, Gilzenberg also promoted wrestling matches in the New Jersey area.

Albano was trained by Soldier Barry and Arnold Skaaland, two veteran area wrestlers, and started competing at very small, local church shows. In 1953, he was recruited by Montreal promoter Eddie Quinn, and made his debut on the big-time circuit in a match against Bob Lazaro.

For several years, Albano languished as a "prelim boy," wrestling on opening matches. His biggest break to date came when Northeast promoter Vincent J. McMahon, owner of what was soon to become WWWF, booked him on his weekly television show in Washington, D.C. Albano was signed on as "enhancement talent"—a nice name for a wrestler sent into the ring to lose to the top stars.

In Albano's case, it wasn't just any top star, but Antonino Rocca, McMahon's number-one drawing card. Lou was soundly thrashed by the high-flying Argentinian, and received $25 for his efforts. But more importantly, he got TV exposure.

At the start of the 1960s, Albano's wrestling career finally started picking up steam after he relocated to Chicago, the site of a highly successful promotion that had benefited from a decade of national TV coverage on the Dumont Network. It was there that Albano and fellow Italian-American competitor Tony Altimore joined forces in a tag team known as the Sicilians.

Playing stereotypical Italian gangster roles similar to the Full-Blooded Italians (FBI), Albano & Altimore wore white fedoras and one black glove, and made frequent references to the Mafia during their interviews. The gimmick succeeded in drawing attention to them, and on June 30, 1961, they won the Midwest Tag Team Championship—appropriately enough, from a duo known as the G-Men, composed of Billy Goelz & Johnny Gilbert.

Not all of the attention drawn to the Sicilians was positive. Legend has it that they were paid a visit by representatives of Chicago mob boss Tony Accaro, who suggested somewhat persuasively that they refrain from making direct mention of the Mafia in their promos. Albano & Altimore toned down the gimmick, but remained the Sicilians—the concept was just too much of a success to abandon.

In 1967, they took their act to WWWF, capturing the U.S. Tag Team Championship from Spiros Arion & Arnold Skaaland in Atlantic City in July. Just three weeks later, they dropped the gold to the team of Arion and WWWF Heavyweight Champion Bruno Sammartino. That was just the beginning of a long association between Albano and the McMahons.

"Albano never claimed to be Lou Thesz," said Freddie Blassie. "He was an average wrestler, but an exceptional talker. That's why Vince Sr. made him a manager. You could bring him out with a protégé who was a complete zero, and in two or three minutes, he'd have you believing that the guy was one of the all-time greats."

Given the fictional rank of "captain," in 1969 Albano became the first of what would eventually become WWWF's "unholy trinity" of classic managers, later to be joined by Blassie and the Grand Wizard. His first protégé was Crusher Verdu, whose feud with Bruno Sammartino reignited WWWF after the temporary loss of television coverage in the late 1960s had nearly killed the company.

"My job as manager," Albano explains, "was getting out there with the hype. I was the one who did it all, putting it together."

By far, Albano's specialty was Tag Teams. In the summer of 1970, he guided the Mongols to the WWWF International Tag Team title, and repeated the feat the following year. Over the next fifteen years, he would duplicate the achievement sixteen times with the WWWF World Tag Team title, making champions out of such tandems as the Valiant Brothers, the Blackjacks, the Executioners, the Yukon Lumberjacks, the Wild Samoans, the Moondogs, and the British Bulldogs.

In addition to his Tag Team glories, Albano managed Pat Patterson, the Magnificent Muraco, and Greg "The Hammer"

Valentine to the Intercontinental Championship. And on January 18, 1971, he shocked the wrestling world to its foundations by leading Ivan Koloff to victory over Sammartino in Madison Square Garden, breaking the Living Legend's seven-year hold on the Heavyweight Championship.

Capt. Lou's success earned him the moniker "The Guiding Light." Adding on poundage as the years went by, he became one of the WWWF's most flamboyant personages. He added to his outrageous image by piercing his cheeks with safety pins, an idea he got from a wino he once spotted in the Bowery (later, he would enhance the visual by hanging rubber bands from the pins).

"He had so much energy," says legendary announcer "Mean" Gene Okerlund. "The name-dropping he would do was just brilliant, those characters he'd come up with—Dr. Rodney Papuffnik, Lanato Bosqueeps Albano, and so forth. In those days, interviews really drove sales for live events. And that was Lou's specialty. He could make up for any lack of speaking experience on the part of the people he managed."

Many of the Captain's eccentricities went beyond his wrestling persona. His indulgences, which included overeating and boozing, were notorious.

"You know, I did occasionally have a few drinks," Albano admits. "I was hell when well, and never sick, mean when I was drinking, drinking a little bit all the time. I'm a legend in my own mind."

"When the matches were over, he'd drag me to one bar after another," remembered Blassie. "If you bought Lou a drink, you'd have a friend for life—because he'd keep coming back to you for a second and a third one. If you opened a saloon, you'd become his cousin.

"Because of his numerous mental defects," Blassie continued, "Albano was probably one of the most entertaining men on television in the early seventies—a cut above even Archie Bunker and Lou Grant. We were in a routine of driving together, and sometimes I thought of him as a little brother—the kind who follows you around and talks in your ear until you want to throw him off a bridge."

After WWWF became World Wrestling Federation and began its mainstream explosion under Vincent K. McMahon in the mid-1980s, Capt. Lou Albano became one of the most unlikely, yet important, parts of that explosion. After striking up a conversation on an airplane with up-and-coming pop star and fellow New Yorker Cyndi Lauper, Albano made appearances in some of her music videos, including "Girls Just Want to Have Fun" and "She-Bop." Through the captain, Lauper developed a relationship with World Wrestling Federation, leading to what was known as "the Rock 'n' Wrestling Connection." Her appearance at *WrestleMania* would enhance this connection, which was controversial to the old school wrestlers.

At first, Capt. Lou played the role of antagonist, insulting Lauper on TV with chauvinistic comments. But he eventually made up with her, and as a result made a dramatic transformation into one of the company's most beloved figures.

He called it quits in 1986 around the same time as Blassie, making way for a new generation of managers. Years later, in 1994, he made a glorious return to World Wrestling Federation, but this was not quite the Albano fans remembered. The Captain had conquered his personal demons and cleaned up his act, dropping 150 pounds in the process. The new, svelte Albano even enjoyed one last championship run, joining with Afa the Wild Samoan to manage the Headshrinkers to yet another Tag Team Championship.

Although mostly inactive in the sport these days, Albano has been known to make appearances on the independent circuit. He also coauthored *The Complete Idiot's Guide to Pro Wrestling* with boxing scribe Bert Randolph Sugar. Once in a while, he has even shown his bearded face on an occasional WWE broadcast. Now, as in his heyday, Capt. Lou Albano remains WWE royalty.

- The Grand Wizard was the first major manager to never have been a wrestler.

- Among the men first brought to WWWF by the Wizard were Don Muraco, Greg Valentine, Ken Patera, and Pat Patterson.

- Among the Grand Wizard's young disciples was a teenaged Paul Heyman.

Of WWWF's "evil trinity" of managers during the 1970s and early '80s, "Classy" Freddie Blassie may have been the most famous; Capt. Lou Albano may have been the most successful; but the Grand Wizard was the most influential.

Decked out in mismatched polyester suits, sequined turbans, and wraparound shades, the Wizard was the "mad genius" of WWWF. What made him even more hateable was the fact that all that bravado was held in the frail-looking body of a man who'd never wrestled a day in his life. In later years, the Grand Wizard "template" would be the inspiration for many managers, and his influence could be seen in men like Jim Cornette and Paul Heyman.

THE GRAND WIZARD

HEIGHT: 5'7"

WEIGHT: 130 lbs.

FROM: Canton, OH

YEARS IN WWE: 1972–83

CAREER HIGHLIGHTS: Manager of the Sheik; manager of two WWWF Heavyweight Champions (Stan Stasiak and Superstar Billy Graham); 1996 WWE Hall of Famer

He was born Ernie Roth in Canton, Ohio, on June 7, 1929. As a young man, Roth tried his hand at radio announcing. Certainly, his gift of gab has its roots in this formative period of his life. But by the beginning of the 1960s, Roth had left radio for another career path.

That path led to the colorful world of professional wrestling. Not to be a wrestler—he was too small for that—but to be a manager, where his diminutive size would be an asset in drawing the ire of fans. He attached himself to one of the hottest performers of the era, the Sheik. Billed as a sadistic wildman from the Middle East, the Sheik terrorized crowds nationwide, taking his act on the road to virtually every territory.

Ironically, Roth, a Jew, was brought in as Muslim manager Abdullah Farouk, with the pretense that the Sheik's wealthy parents had sent Farouk to the United States to handle their son's career. The pair was an instant hit. Roth found it easy to whip fans into a frenzy by interfering in his charge's matches, a relatively rare tactic at that time.

For years, Abdullah Farouk was the exclusive manager of the Sheik. But as the 1970s began, they went their separate ways— although Roth would occasionally return to the Sheik's home territory in Detroit to reunite briefly with his first protégé.

In 1972 Ernie Roth was brought into WWWF under a new name—the Grand Wizard of Wrestling. He almost immediately led the formidable duo of Mr. Fuji & Professor Toru Tanaka to the World Tag Team Championship in June, and managed to keep the championships on his men for nearly a year. He duplicated the feat the following year with the same team.

"He was a great guy," remembers fellow manager Arnold Skaaland. "A great talker. He could talk for people who couldn't talk. And he liked being hated. That was his job, and he liked it. He liked to incite people. The more they booed him, the better he liked it."

Another of his early protégés was Stan Stasiak, and the Wizard wasted no time in guiding him to the WWWF Heavyweight Championship, which he won from Pedro Morales in Philadelphia

The Wiz and Professor Toru Tanaka with referee Danny Bartfield.

on December 1, 1973. That reign would last a mere nine days before it was ended in Madison Square Garden by Bruno Sammartino, but the Grand Wizard had established himself as a force to be reckoned with on the WWWF scene.

"Like me, he didn't memorize lines before his interviews," said Blassie in his autobiography, *Listen, You Pencil Neck Geeks*. "Whatever was in his mind just flowed out."

Being paired with the Grand Wizard was a major boon for any competitor, and his services were enjoyed by such dastardly individuals as Stan Hansen, Ernie Ladd, Ox Baker, and Killer Kowalski. But his greatest charge was Superstar Billy Graham, the charismatic and colorful muscleman who toppled Sammartino from the championship position in 1977 and proceeded to go on a ten-month tear as titleholder.

"Vince Sr., at my first television appearance [for WWWF], introduced me to the Grand Wizard, and said, 'He's gonna be with you, he's one of the best mouthpieces in the business,' " recalls Graham. "The Wizard and I worked really perfectly together because he would pull off my T-shirts , take my jewelry off, my sunglasses off, and it worked out. We really complemented each other. He was great, just incredible to work with. It was so easy, because he complemented me with all his goofy valet stuff."

Both flamboyant and comfortable with a microphone, the two were a perfect fit. When Graham's reign was stopped by Bob Backlund, the Wizard made it his goal to destroy the pure and wholesome new champion. Ridiculing him with such monikers as "Opie" and "Howdy Doody," he brought in challenger after challenger, but none could ever get the job done.

In the last years of his career, the Grand Wizard led both Ken Patera (1980) and the Magnificent Muraco (1981) to the brand-new Intercontinental Championship. But it all came to a sudden and tragic end when on October 12, 1983, "The Grand Wizard" Ernie Roth died of a heart attack at age fifty-four.

Passing away mere months short of World Wrestling Federation's national expansion the following year, the Grand Wizard missed out on enjoying the kind of national, mainstream notoriety many of his colleagues would soon experience. Still, to the loyal fan base in the Northeast, he would be remembered as the object of their ultimate hatred. And he wouldn't have wanted it any other way.

- The modern style of Cage match, where competitors must escape the cage, was developed for Blassie in Los Angeles in the 1960s.

- A popular urban legend has it that Blassie's real last name was Blassman and that he was Jewish. Both are untrue.

- Blassie's name is dropped in the REM song "Man on the Moon."

One of the biggest-drawing performers in wrestling history, "Classy" Freddie Blassie enjoyed a career of rare longevity that spanned several incarnations. From wrestler to manager to good-will ambassador, Blassie truly was one of a kind. As he worked with four generations of McMahons, there was perhaps no one that family respected more. The cult following he gathered over the years was and still is a tribute to the indelible mark left on popular culture by the self-proclaimed King of Men.

Blassie was born in St. Louis, Missouri, on February 8, 1918. Even in those days, the city of St. Louis was a big wrestling town, and the young Blassie often attended the matches. He began his

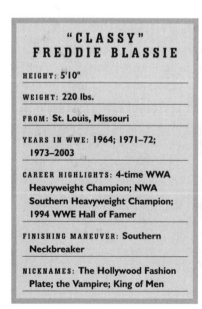

"CLASSY" FREDDIE BLASSIE

HEIGHT: 5'10"

WEIGHT: 220 lbs.

FROM: St. Louis, Missouri

YEARS IN WWE: 1964; 1971–72; 1973–2003

CAREER HIGHLIGHTS: 4-time WWA Heavyweight Champion; NWA Southern Heavyweight Champion; 1994 WWE Hall of Famer

FINISHING MANEUVER: Southern Neckbreaker

NICKNAMES: The Hollywood Fashion Plate; the Vampire; King of Men

own wrestling career not in arenas but in carnivals—a throwback to pro wrestling's roots in the nineteenth century.

While working in the carnival, he coined the term *pencil neck geek*, which he used to describe the carnival's actual sideshow geek. That term would eventually be used by Blassie as a term of derision for fans, opponents, and the public at large. Eventually, it would become part of popular American jargon.

In the late 1930s, Blassie spent a brief time wrestling in the Northeast for promoter Jess McMahon, grandfather of WWE chairman Vincent K. McMahon. During World War II, he served in the U.S. Navy, seeing action in the South Pacific. Following the war, he tried to parlay his experience into a catchy gimmick, calling himself "Sailor" Fred Blassie. The experiment failed to attract much attention.

"Even when I'd wrestle clean, I'd get booed," remembered Blassie in his 2003 autobiography, *Listen, You Pencil Neck Geeks*. "In 1956, I finally said, 'The hell with this. If these idiots want to boo, I'll give them something to boo about.' "

Thus, a transformation occurred that would make Freddie Blassie one of wrestling's unforgettable characters. Bleaching his hair blond in the fashion of Gorgeous George, the most well known competitor of the day, he rechristened himself "Classy" Freddie Blassie. Openly courting the disdain of the fans, he would brag about his power over women, and ridicule the "pathetic inbred hicks" he saw in the stands. Before long, he was one of the sport's most hated villains.

The downside of attracting this kind of attention was the all-too-real physical danger it often put him in. Over the years, Blassie would be stabbed, assaulted with acid, and even had his brand-new Cadillac set on fire. But to him, it was well worth the risk.

Blassie captured the NWA Southern Heavyweight Championship numerous times in the late 1950s. The next decade saw him become a fixture on the Los Angeles wrestling scene, where he would achieve his greatest success as an in-ring competitor. He won the WWA Heavyweight title, then one of the top titles in the nation, on four occasions. While attempting to regain the title from Japanese legend Rikidozan, he added a new dimension to his growing mystique, in the process becoming one of the most famous American competitors in Japanese wrestling history.

Filing his teeth during interviews, he would brag about drawing blood from his enemies, and when he went on to do just that, the Japanese press dubbed him "The Vampire." During a highly publicized match with Rikidozan that was viewed by a record-breaking TV audience in Japan, several elderly viewers are believed to have actually died of heart attacks while watching Blassie's blood-soaked brutality unfold.

In 1964, Blassie came to the World Wide Wrestling Federation for the first time, to challenge Heavyweight Champion Bruno Sammartino. He headlined Madison Square Garden against Bruno twice and also had high-profile MSG matches against fellow future Hall of Famers Bobo Brazil and Pedro Morales.

"I wanted to wrestle Bruno in the worst way," Blassie recalled. "In the WWA, I was recognized as the World Champion in California, Hawaii, Asia, and a few places in the Midwest. Sammartino defended his WWWF title in arenas from Washington, D.C., to Maine. Our confrontation was considered something of a dream match."

Although Blassie remained reviled on the East Coast, his charismatic persona had begun winning over fans in sunny California by the late 1960s. By the end of the decade, he was the most popular wrestler in the Los Angeles territory. As the 1970s began, he became embroiled in his most famous feud, with John Tolos.

The Blassie/Tolos feud took off in 1971, reaching a head on August 27, when the two met head-on in the Los Angeles Coliseum. It was the first pro wrestling event to be carried on closed circuit, and drew 25,847 to the Coliseum—an L.A. record that still stands.

"He had such tremendous credibility as a wrestler," says "Mean" Gene Okerlund. "In southern California, his name was as big as Gorgeous George. He was revered, and he stayed around for so long. There was something fans could see that made him a main-event world-class wrestler."

Without missing a beat, Blassie returned to WWWF, where he was still a hated man. He challenged Heavyweight Champion Pedro Morales in back-to-back main events at Madison Square Garden, and also tangled with the immensely popular Chief Jay Strongbow. By this point, Blassie's wrestling career was winding down. He was fifty-three, and many athletic commissions would no longer sanction him to compete.

Thus began the next chapter of his storied career, which would bring him even greater fame nationwide. In 1973, he was hired full-time by Vincent J. McMahon as a manager, joining the already established Capt. Lou Albano and the Grand Wizard. For the rest of his life, Fred Blassie would remain in the employ of the McMahon family and WWE.

His first protégé was Nikolai Volkoff. His charges included some of the most despicable individuals to ever set foot in WWE, men like Spiros Arion, Blackjack Mulligan, and George "The Animal" Steele. He specialized in anti-American heels like Mr. Fuji & Professor Toru Tanaka, who he led to the World Tag Team title in 1977. With his trademark cane, Blassie was always ready to lend an interfering hand to help his men win out.

"As a manager, he was a natural on his feet," says Okerlund. "Back in that era, guys had to ad-lib by the seat of their pants. For him, that was easy. He always knew how to get himself across."

One protégé of note was a twenty-five-year-old from Tampa, Florida, whom Vincent J. McMahon dubbed Hulk Hogan. In 1979 Blassie took on the rookie Hogan, then a hated rulebreaker, and gave him his first exposure to World Wrestling Federation fans.

But Blassie's fame by this time had spread beyond wrestling. He had achieved bona fide cult status, as can be seen by the immortal novelty songs he recorded in 1975: "Pencil Neck Geek" and "Blassie—King of Men." He even attracted the attention of America's most eccentric comedian of the time, Andy Kaufman.

Kaufman was fascinated with wrestling, and Blassie was one of his major idols. The unorthodox entertainer convinced him to take part in a unique film that came to be called *My Breakfast with Blassie*. A spoof of the art-house film *My Dinner with Andre* (not the Giant), the movie depicted Kaufman and Blassie having breakfast and sharing bizarre anecdotes at a popular L.A. diner.

"I can't say I understood the point of *My Breakfast with Blassie*," admitted the King of Men. "All we did was talk about bullshit. I guess there must have been a lot of Andy Kaufmans out there, if people were willing to pay for a movie ticket, just to hear my opinions about day-to-day garbage."

Blassie and Kaufman remained close friends for the remainder of the comedian's life, and Blassie even sat in the front row with the family at Kaufman's funeral in 1984.

Blassie reached the pinnacle of his managerial career on December 26, 1983, when, calling himself "Ayatollah" Blassie, he led the Iron Sheik to a controversial victory over Bob Backlund for the World Wrestling Federation Championship.

With the era of *Hulkamania*, Blassie's managerial run soon came to a close. He managed the Iron Sheik & Nikolai Volkoff to the World Tag Team Championship at the first *WrestleMania* in 1985, and several months later, stepped away from his on-air role for good. His body was breaking down, and the constant travel was doing him no good.

Settling into a position as goodwill ambassador, Blassie remained a part of the World Wrestling Federation family. In addition to his charitable activities, he occasionally did voiceovers on WWE telecasts, and even made rare appearances now and then on TV.

In 2003 Blassie's autobiography, *Listen, You Pencil Neck Geeks*, was published. To help promote it, a wheelchair-bound but no-less-determined King of Men made his final WWE appearance, on the May 12 edition of *Raw*.

Just days later, on June 2, 2003, at approximately 8:30 P.M., Freddie Blassie, one of WWE's most enduring and respected legends, passed away at age eighty-five. The legacy he left behind will always be cherished by those within WWE, as well as by the countless fans who remember the exploits of the one and only "Hollywood Fashion Plate."

"To a certain extent, Freddie represented my father to me, the era that my father came from," wrote Vince McMahon in the introduction to Blassie's autobiography. "I remember how much my father admired Freddie because he was a ballsy son of a bitch who gave so much. When he was on your team, there wasn't anything he wouldn't do for you. I'm honored that my family meant so much to this exceptional man."

AND THE CROWD GOES WILD:

HEROES OF THE RING

- Gorilla's personalized license plate read "KAYFABE," a reference to pro wrestling's code of secrecy.

- Monsoon was Vincent J. McMahon's original choice to succeed him as company owner.

- Fellow wrestler Hard Boiled Haggerty played a fictionalized version of Gorilla Monsoon in the 1984 comedy *Micki & Maude*.

Robert Marella entered the wrestling business in 1959, working for northeastern promoters Vincent J. McMahon and Joseph "Toots" Mondt. He debuted as Gorilla Monsoon, a "former Asiatic Champion" billed as hailing from Manchuria. With manager Wild Red Berry at his side to do all the talking, Monsoon was instantly one of the most hated heels in the country.

He was born in 1937 in Rochester, New York, to parents of Italian descent. Prior to his pro career, he excelled as an amateur wrestler, and was a standout at Ithaca University, where he majored in physical education. He finished second in the NCAA championships in 1959, and an 18-second pin remains the quickest in the school's history. He also set school records in discus and shot put

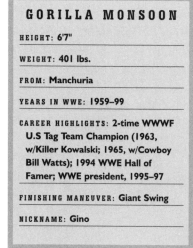

GORILLA MONSOON

HEIGHT: 6'7"

WEIGHT: 401 lbs.

FROM: Manchuria

YEARS IN WWE: 1959–99

CAREER HIGHLIGHTS: 2-time WWWF U.S Tag Team Champion (1963, w/Killer Kowalski; 1965, w/Cowboy Bill Watts); 1994 WWE Hall of Famer; WWE president, 1995–97

FINISHING MANEUVER: Giant Swing

NICKNAME: Gino

(Marella was inducted into the Ithaca College Sports Hall of Fame in 1973).

Shortly thereafter, he made the transition to the professional ranks. His pro wrestling debut occurred at the Rochester War Memorial Arena in the summer of 1959, where 6,000 fans saw him quickly pin Pauncho Lopez.

On November 14, 1963, Monsoon teamed with fellow rule-breaker Killer Kowalski to win the U.S. Tag Team Championship from Skull Murphy & Brute Bernard in Washington, D.C. Then, on November 18, with his first professional title wrapped around his waist, Monsoon stepped into the ring with Heavyweight Champion Bruno Sammartino at the old Madison Square Garden in a match that both men would later cite as the toughest of their careers. It went the full 90-minute time limit without a winner decided.

Monsoon & Kowalski lost their Tag Team title to the Tolos Brothers on December 28 in Teaneck, New Jersey. He regained the U.S. Tag Team Championship in April 1965, this time teaming with Cowboy Bill Watts to defeat Gene Kiniski & Waldo Von Erich in D.C. The duo dropped the title to the Miller Brothers three months later.

In 1969, Gorilla Monsoon was mercilessly attacked on television by the Sheik, a wrestler even more vicious and hated than he. Coming to his rescue was former archrival Sammartino; thus was Monsoon reborn as a "good guy," a role he filled for the remainder of his career. He dropped Red Berry, and toned down the "Manchurian" gimmick. The 1970s saw Monsoon go through a complete reversal; one of the most despised heels of the previous decade became one of the most beloved babyfaces of the next one.

The change in roles brought Gorilla Monsoon a little closer in resemblance to Robert Marella, the warm family man. He was always supremely appreciative of the fans who paid their hard-earned money to see him. His respect for the fans translated into respect for his craft, and Monsoon always prided himself on giving the people their money's worth.

The most high-profile incident of Monsoon's wrestling career

Mr. Fuji vs. Gorilla Monsoon.

occurred in 1976 at a TV taping in Hamburg, Pennsylvania, when he was challenged by Heavyweight Boxing Champion Muhammad Ali. The challenge resulted in Monsoon hoisting the champ into an airplane spin and slamming him to the canvas.

In 1981, Monsoon officially retired from the ring. Vincent K. McMahon, who had bought the company from his father, put Monsoon behind the mic, making him the company's top play-by-play man. Once WWE began to go national in the mid-1980s, Monsoon was introduced to wrestling fans across the country and around the world, many of whom had never seen him before. For close to fifteen years, Monsoon's broadcasting duties included syndicated programming, Pay-Per-Views, and local cable broadcasts on channels such as the MSG Network. He and Jesse "The Body" Ventura are considered by many to have been the greatest commentary team in the history of televised wrestling. Monsoon also formed a winning duo with Bobby "The Brain" Heenan, playing the exasperated straight man to great effect.

"He was one of my best friends," says Heenan. "We'd argue, we'd fight each other back and forth, but we had mutual respect for each other."

Another role of Monsoon's—one that he had occupied during his wrestling years as well—was trusted confidant and adviser to the McMahon family. He had been a business partner of Vincent J. McMahon, and worked behind the scenes at many events. In this capacity, he was known for being helpful and encouraging to all those around him, always accessible and considerate, yet firm when the situation called for it.

In his home life, Monsoon was known as a kind, gentle man. He enjoyed cooking Italian food—he prided himself on his lasagna—and made a tradition of playing Santa Claus for his kids.

In 1994, Monsoon was inducted into the WWE Hall of Fame. That same year also saw an unthinkable tragedy for the Marella family as Monsoon's son, referee Joey Marella, was killed in an auto accident on the New Jersey Turnpike returning home from a wrestling event. Some have traced Monsoon's failing health back to this incident.

Gorilla Monsoon was named WWE president in 1995. In his role as president, Monsoon played a key role in many story lines. But by 1997, his health had begun to deteriorate. He was suffering from diabetes and experiencing heart problems as well. He stepped down as president and faded from the scene at last. In 1998 he suffered a stroke, and his condition swiftly worsened from then on. His last public appearance was at *WrestleMania XV* in Philadelphia on March 28, 1999. He was introduced as one of the ringside judges for the Brawl for All Championship match between Butterbean and Bart Gunn. Monsoon received a huge standing ovation from the crowd, but the truth was obvious. The pale, gaunt Robert Marella who smiled weakly to the crowd that night was a far cry from the rampaging Gorilla Monsoon of old.

On September 19, 1999, Marella had a mild heart attack. He made it through, but complications from the attack caused his kidneys to fail. On the morning of October 4, 1999, Robert Marella passed away at the age of sixty-two.

"That was a great loss, both to the business, and to me personally," says Bobby Heenan.

For forty years, Gorilla Monsoon entertained audiences and dedicated himself to the business like few others. Almost no one was ever a member of WWE for a longer period of time. Robert "Gorilla Monsoon" Marella will always be remembered as one of the great ones, and stands out as a true giant, both in size and reputation.

- Strongbow served as campaign manager for Gorgeous George when the Gorgeous One ran for president of the United States in 1952.

- Strongbow's Italian-American heritage caused fellow *paisan* Lou Albano to joke that he was a member of the "Woppaho" tribe.

- Chief Jay made a cameo appearance in the 1984 movie *Micki and Maude*, starring the late Dudley Moore.

If you had to make a list of the most popular WWE competitors never to hold a singles championship in WWE, Chief Jay Strongbow would be at the top of that list. In the 1970s and early '80s, he was among the most passionately adored Superstars, a regular on nearly every show the company put on. But Strongbow was content to soak in the adulation of the crowds as opposed to title glory.

Strongbow was probably the most well known wrestler to take on the tried-and-true Native American persona. A staple introduced by Chief Thunderbird in the early 1930s, the Indian grappler clad in traditional tribal gear is one of the most iconic symbols of professional wrestling through the generations.

CHIEF JAY STRONGBOW

HEIGHT: 6'2"

WEIGHT: 265 lbs.

FROM: Pawhuska, OK

YEARS IN WWE: 1970–79; 1982–95

CAREER HIGHLIGHTS: 4-time WWWF World Tag Team Champion (1972, 1976, 1982, 1982); 2-time NWA World Tag Team Champion (Florida & Mid-America versions); 1994 WWE Hall of Famer

FINISHING MANEUVERS: Tomahawk Chop; Indian deathlock

Yet pro wrestling has always been part illusion. Although Native American wrestlers could often boast an actual Indian heritage, just as often it was nothing more than a well-played gimmick. Chief Jay Strongbow was of the latter grouping.

He was born Joseph Scarpa in 1928, to Italian-American parents. Although he achieved his greatest fame as "Native American" Jay Strongbow, that was only during the latter phase of his almost-forty-year career in the sport. For many years, he wrestled under his given name.

Joltin' Joe Scarpa debuted in L.A. in the late 1940s. The L.A. territory was one of the nation's hot spots, thanks to the presence of Hollywood. Ironically, Scarpa was mentored by Don Eagle, the most successful and popular Native American grappling star up to that point in time. Another major headliner who would have an effect on the young Scarpa was the Toast of the Coast himself, Gorgeous George—then one of the most high-profile TV stars in America.

Learning about the showmanship aspect of the business from such colorful legends, Scarpa headed south, where he would spend more than a decade eking out a living. He went to work in Memphis in the late 1950s. He achieved his first notoriety there, and was even given a shot at NWA World Champion Buddy Rogers in August 1961.

Scarpa also spent some time in Florida, as well as Alabama's Gulf Coast territory, where he won his first title—the NWA Gulf Coast Championship—in 1960. And in Georgia, Scarpa challenged Lou Thesz for the NWA World title at Marietta in 1964. He won the NWA Georgia Heavyweight title in 1969 to close out the decade.

The 1960s had taken Scarpa a lot further than he had been during his California years, but he certainly wasn't about to go down as one of the all-time greats. Had it not been for his decision to head north to WWWF, Joe Scarpa would likely have become a relatively minor footnote in the history of southern wrestling.

But at age forty-two, Scarpa stumbled upon a gimmick that would place his name—well, not his actual name—among the sport's elite. Taking inspiration most likely from the name of longtime L.A. matchmaker Jules Strongbow, Scarpa and WWWF kingpin Vincent J. McMahon came up with the name "Chief Jay Strongbow," and transformed Scarpa into a Native American—complete with war bonnet, beads, leather vest, and everything else that went along with the concept.

He took to the part so well that fans were soon clamoring for him. His Tomahawk Chops could bring crowds to their feet, and fans knew that when the Chief broke into his Indian war dance, the end was near.

Strongbow was a WWWF regular for the entire decade. He won his first of an eventual four WWWF World Tag titles in 1972, teaming with African-American Superstar Sonny King to beat Baron Mikel Scicluna & King Curtis Iaukea. Strongbow & King were the first interracial World Tag Team Champions, and that feat would not be duplicated in a major promotion for over twenty years.

At a time when Strongbow's career should have been winding down, it was hotter than ever, especially in the minds of the majority of northeastern fans who had never seen him compete as Joe Scarpa. He was experiencing far greater success as Strongbow—and making far more money—than he had ever known before.

"He was a decent guy, but very thrifty," recalled Freddie Blassie in his autobiography, *Listen, You Pencil Neck Geeks*. "If he made a dime, he saved eleven cents of it. When the boys wanted to rib him, they'd ask how much he paid for his hotel room. After he answered, they'd claim to have found a cheaper place down the road. The thought of another guy squirreling away more shekels killed Strongbow, and he'd hit the ceiling. I remember when he bought a farm outside Atlanta. There was a lake on the property, and he stocked it with fish. Then, he charged fishermen to use the water. Which I guess is all right, it's just not my cup of tea."

"Thrifty" or not, Strongbow didn't have to worry about where his money was coming from, because before long he was among the top handful of WWWF fan favorites. Some might argue that his popularity was second only to Heavyweight Champions like Bruno Sammartino and Pedro Morales.

Johnny Valiant at Strongbow's mercy.

In 1974, Strongbow formed a dream team with Sammartino, taking on Tag Team Champions Jimmy & Johnny Valiant. "Handsome" Jimmy Valiant in particular had raised the ire of Strongbow, due to the fact that he had formerly been his friend and ally, only to turn against him and join forces with his villainous "brother." Strongbow & Sammartino opposed the Valiants in three main events at Madison Square Garden that are remembered for their brutality and close competition.

The Valiant/Strongbow pattern would be repeated several times over the next few years, with great success. At the end of 1974, Strongbow found himself embroiled in a feud with Spiros Arion. A former fan favorite and a Tag Team ally of the Chief, Arion viciously turned against him and knocked him unconscious, disrespectfully shoving his ceremonial feathers in his mouth. This was the ultimate outrage for Strongbow, and sparked a heated rivalry.

By the summer of 1976, Strongbow had a new Tag Team partner, another part-time Indian named Billy White Wolf (who resurfaced fifteen years later as the Iraqi General Adnan). The duo chased World Tag Team Champions the Executioners for the remainder of the year, but it was only after the masked champions were stripped of the gold that Strongbow & White Wolf were able to win it in a tournament final. They held the title for eight months, until Olympic strongman Ken Patera put White Wolf on the shelf with an injury, forcing the team to vacate their crowns.

During the late 1970s, in his last major singles feud, Strongbow had his leg broken by brash young heel Greg "The Hammer" Valentine and his patented figure-four leglock. The summer of 1979 saw Strongbow and Valentine collide in all sorts of bouts, including the dreaded Indian Strap match at MSG, soon after which the Chief walked away from the territory, having stayed much longer than most ever did, thanks to his intense popularity.

Jay Strongbow traveled to Puerto Rico in 1980, competing in Carlos Colon's World Wrestling Council (WWC). He was also brought into Georgia Championship Wrestling by Wahoo McDaniel, the other major Indian star of the era, and the two formed a brief but memorable alliance.

When he returned to World Wrestling Federation in 1982, it was as a Tag Team competitor. This time, his partner was a wrestler named Jules Strongbow (not to be confused with the promoter), who was billed as the Chief's brother. They won the Tag Team Championship twice from Mr. Fuji & Mr. Saito. Their second reign (Chief Jay's last) was ended in March 1983 by the Wild Samoans.

Chief Jay began to slide down the ladder of contention. He was now fifty-five years old, and time was catching up with him. Soon he was relegated to lower- to mid-card matchups, frequently losing to up-and-coming grapplers like Sgt. Slaughter, Cowboy Bob Orton Jr., and Paul Orndorff. It was the era of *Hulkamania,* and the past-his-prime Strongbow no longer had a place in the rapidly expanding scheme of things.

He retired from competition in 1985 and was given a backstage position as a road agent. His main responsibility included recruiting new talent, and he would frequently attend independent shows to scout prospects.

In 1994, the Chief stepped back into the spotlight as the manager of Tatanka, a new Native American Superstar who looked to him for guidance. However, history would repeat itself one last time for Strongbow, when Tatanka turned his back on him and sold out to the "Million Dollar Man," Ted DiBiase. Not long after, Strongbow stepped down from his office job and left the business for good. He settled down in Georgia, where he still resides.

He may not have been Native American by blood, but don't tell that to the thousands of fans who sat glued to his every move all those years. Regardless of whether he was Navajo or Napolitano, Chief Jay Strongbow embodied the passion and fighting spirit that made him one of WWE's most beloved figures ever.

- **Andre the Giant holds the world's record for most beers consumed in a single sitting.**

- **Andre drew the ire of *The Princess Bride* director Rob Reiner by keeping his fellow actors up late with all-night parties.**

- **Andre's first wrestling name, Jean Ferre, was derived from a legendary French giant.**

He was the largest athlete the world had ever seen, and professional wrestling's most famous attraction throughout the 1970s and much of the '80s. Standing seven-foot-four and weighing between 475 and 540 pounds over the course of his career, he earned his nickname of "The Eighth Wonder of the World."

Andre Rene Rousimoff was born to Russian immigrants in a small French village on May 19, 1946. By the time he was twelve, the boy stood six-three and weighed in at 200 pounds. This was due to the fact that he was born with acromegaly, a disorder that causes the bones to grow at an accelerated rate, and to continue to grow beyond the age of physical maturity, normally causing death by late middle age.

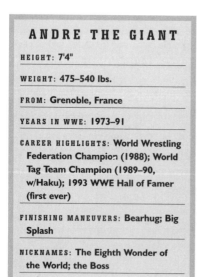

ANDRE THE GIANT

HEIGHT: 7'4"

WEIGHT: 475–540 lbs.

FROM: Grenoble, France

YEARS IN WWE: 1973–91

CAREER HIGHLIGHTS: World Wrestling Federation Champion (1988); World Tag Team Champion (1989–90, w/Haku); 1993 WWE Hall of Famer (first ever)

FINISHING MANEUVERS: Bearhug; Big Splash

NICKNAMES: The Eighth Wonder of the World; the Boss

Determined to use his abnormal size to his advantage, Andre entered the world of professional wrestling as a very young man. Instantly, fans were taken with the young man's incredible size wherever he went. He was a real-life giant among men, and people were willing to pay just for a chance to see him. As early as 1969, he was already making a name for himself in wrestling promotions throughout Europe and French Canada, calling himself "Jean Ferre" to accentuate his French roots. By 1971, he was on the road to becoming a phenomenon in Japan, where he won the prestigious IWA round robin tournament, finishing ahead of revered grapplers Billy Robinson and Karl Gotch.

At the beginning of 1973, the twenty-seven-year-old Rousimoff came under the wing of Vincent J. McMahon and World Wide Wrestling Federation, the most dominant territory in the nation at the time thanks in part to its exclusive rights to New York's Madison Square Garden. McMahon christened the former Jean Ferre with the name he would forever be remembered by—Andre the Giant—and debuted him at MSG on March 26, 1973. Andre and McMahon also came to an agreement whereby WWWF would act as the Giant's "booking agency," sending him out to wrestling territories all over the world on loan. Though the company would change dramatically, Andre would remain with the McMahon family for the next twenty years.

"He was famous as soon as he got there," says fellow WWE Hall of Famer Killer Kowalski. "The people turned out to see him squash and beat up everybody."

In an era when the sport was very regionalized, Andre the Giant became one of the rare exceptions: a performer who was at the top of the card wherever he went, a major star who was known to fans in every territory. From Florida to California, Texas to Michigan, Mexico to Australia, his arrival was an epic event. He challenged NWA World Champions like Harley Race and Ric Flair, and even held the NWA U.S. Tag Team title with fellow mega-star Dusty Rhodes on two occasions. His crossover celebrity status was such that he appeared as a guest on the *Tonight Show,* and even had a cameo role on the *Six-Million-Dollar Man* playing Bigfoot.

Andre the Giant vs. Butcher Vachon.

Every few months, Andre would return "home" to the Northeast. His rivalries with the likes of "Big Cat" Ernie Ladd, Don Leo Jonathan, and Blackjack Mulligan are the stuff of legend. At WWE's 1976 Shea Stadium event, he engaged in a boxer vs. wrestler confrontation with Chuck Wepner, in which he hurled the "Bayonne Bleeder" out of the ring and into the third row. Four years later, he had his first encounter with Hulk Hogan when the Federation returned to Shea. One of the most memorable rivalries of the time was with Killer Khan, who broke Andre's ankle in 1981, leading to the infamous Mongolian Stretcher match between the two. Through it all, Andre maintained an incredible undefeated streak the likes of which has never been seen before or since.

"This was his life," says WWE referee and Andre's onetime confidant, Tim White. "He knew that he could get in the ring with somebody, and make or break them. His criteria was that you had to respect the business."

Andre's personality was fittingly larger-than-life. He enjoyed spreading his money around, taking his friends out for all-night parties. Some believed the reason to be that Andre knew he would not live to old age, and so he wanted to enjoy himself while he was still alive. Although he rarely let it be known, Andre could be sensitive about his condition. In short, he wanted to be seen as something more than an oddity or sideshow attraction.

By the mid-1980s, Andre's condition was beginning to take its toll on his body. He was slowing down and putting on more and more weight. Still, he remained an integral part of the World Wrestling Federation's national expansion during the era of *Hulkamania*. He was victorious over Big John Studd in the Bodyslam Challenge at the first *WrestleMania* in 1985, and added to his record for most battle royals won by surviving just such a match the following year at *WrestleMania 2*.

His career took an alarming turn in 1987 when, just returned after starring in the motion picture *The Princess Bride,* he turned on his longtime friend Hulk Hogan and hired Bobby "The Brain" Heenan as his manager. The result was his first-ever shot at World Wrestling Federation Championship. With 93,173 fans in attendance (a record that stands to this day), Andre clashed with the Hulkster at *WrestleMania III* in the biggest match of all time. The result was the end of the Giant's fifteen-year undefeated streak.

Andre did finally win the title from Hogan in a controversial match the following year, only to give it up moments later. He also held the World Tag Team title with Haku for a few months in 1990. But much more than those accomplishments, Andre will be remembered for the years he reigned supreme as the most famous Superstar wrestling had ever produced. He finally succumbed to his lifelong illness in 1993 at the age of forty-six, and shortly thereafter became the first inductee of the WWE Hall of Fame—truly a fitting honor for the one and only Andre the Giant, the Eighth Wonder of the World.

"It's been thirteen years since he died," remembers friend and former manager Arnold Skaaland. "And sometimes I feel like he's still here."

- During his original run as Heavyweight Champion, Backlund could neither read nor write.

- Backlund replaced his Atomic Kneedrop finisher with the cross-face chicken wing to avoid wear and tear on his knees.

- Backlund competed in title unification matches with NWA Champions Harley Race and Ric Flair, and AWA Champion Nick Bockwinkel.

Backlund was wrestling's last World Champion in the classic mold of early pre-WWE titleholders like Ed "Strangler" Lewis and Lou Thesz. He didn't use a gimmick, he didn't play a character, he was simply a wrestler, and a damn good one. A master of the defensive style, Backlund held the Heavyweight title for nearly six years.

The length of his first, great reign is second only to Sammartino's first reign in all of WWE history. In terms of pure grappling skill, no other champion can touch him, with the notable exception of Kurt Angle. It seemed like no one would ever be able to stop him, and it took his own manager literally throwing in the towel to finally get the gold off him.

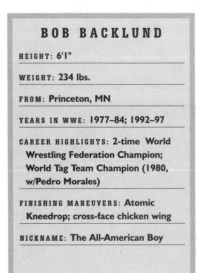

BOB BACKLUND

HEIGHT: 6'1"

WEIGHT: 234 lbs.

FROM: Princeton, MN

YEARS IN WWE: 1977–84; 1992–97

CAREER HIGHLIGHTS: 2-time World Wrestling Federation Champion; World Tag Team Champion (1980, w/Pedro Morales)

FINISHING MANEUVERS: Atomic Kneedrop; cross-face chicken wing

NICKNAME: The All-American Boy

Born August 14, 1950, in Princeton, Minnesota, Backlund first took to wrestling while still in school. He was a high school standout, and took his skills to the next level after he enrolled at North Dakota State University in 1968. There, he attained a heavyweight wrestling championship in NCAA Division II competition.

Despite getting to college based on his outstanding athletic merits, at the time Backlund was actually illiterate. It would not be until years later that he accomplished the impressive feat of teaching himself to read and write. This would help Backlund to one day enter the political arena and run for public office, proving that no obstacle was too great for him to overcome.

But first, he had to make a living for himself. Despite his soft-spoken demeanor, Backlund decided to try his hand at wrestling professionally. Trained for the ring by the likes of Dory Funk Jr., Terry Funk, and Verne Gagne, Backlund debuted in 1974 in Gagne's American Wrestling Association, based in the Midwest. During these early years, he also competed in the NWA's Florida and Georgia territories.

Backlund's white-bread, All-American look and style attracted the attention of Vincent J. McMahon, who was looking for a new Superstar around which to build his World Wide Wrestling Federation. Traditionally, the WWWF Championship had been kept on competitors like Bruno Sammartino and Pedro Morales, who appealed to the Northeast's ethnic fan base. But McMahon was looking to go in a different direction, and hoped that Bob Backlund would be the man for the job.

Billed as the "All-American Boy," Backlund debuted in WWWF in the spring of 1977 under the tutelage of Arnold Skaaland, who was also the manager of WWWF Heavyweight Champion Bruno Sammartino. Shortly after Backlund's debut, however, Bruno was dethroned by the brash, flamboyant Superstar Billy Graham.

Backlund and Graham were on complete opposite ends of the wrestling spectrum as far as their personas, but it was obvious from the start that a match between the two was brewing. Slowly but surely, as 1977 turned into 1978, Backlund compiled win after win, and no matter how much Graham and his obnoxious man-

Bob Backlund vs. Ric Flair.

ager the Grand Wizard derided the unassuming challenger, he was working his way into top contention.

The bout took place on February 20, 1978, in Madison Square Garden, and in just under fifteen minutes, Bob Backlund emerged as the new WWWF Heavyweight Champion, ending the Superstar's ten-month reign of terror. But Graham wasn't about to give up without a fight, and challenged Backlund mightily in two more consecutive main events at the Garden. The first was stopped when Backlund was too bloodied to continue, and the second was a brutal Steel Cage match won by the champion.

With Graham behind him, Backlund embarked on one of the longest championship reigns in history. Only Sammartino, Thesz, and Gagne can claim to have held a World title longer. For nearly six years, WWWF's "unholy trinity" of managers, "Classy" Freddie Blassie, Capt. Lou Albano, and the Grand Wizard, brought in as many savage and sadistic challengers as they could find in a quest to destroy Backlund and all he stood for. Men like Ken Patera, Ivan Koloff, "Big Cat" Ernie Ladd, Sgt. Slaughter, Stan Hansen, George "The Animal" Steele, the Magnificent Muraco, Adrian Adonis, Jesse "The Body" Ventura, and Big John Studd all lined up for their chance. Through it all, the squeaky-clean Backlund kept his sportsmanship and his championship status intact.

But the Backlund reign was certainly not without its share of controversy. In the fall of 1978, he was the victim of a shocking betrayal by onetime ally High Chief Peter Maivia (grandfather of The Rock). The following year, while defending the championship in Japan, he was defeated by Japanese legend Antonio Inoki but quickly regained the title. The title switch was never acknowledged in the United States and WWWF continued to recognize Backlund without interruption.

In 1979 Backlund was met by his most tenacious challenger, WWWF North American Champion Pat Patterson. The two men headlined Madison Square Garden four times in a row, a unique feat that had never been done before, and hasn't since.

Backlund joined forces with former WWWF Champion Pedro Morales in August 1980 to take on World Tag Team Champions the Wild Samoans in a mega-event held in New York's Shea Stadium. The dream duo emerged with the Tag Team gold, but were forced to relinquish the championship shortly thereafter due to the prohibition against individuals holding more than one title simultaneously.

Toward the end of his reign, in 1982, Backlund stood up to the challenge of aerial master Jimmy "Superfly" Snuka. In one memorable encounter in particular, Snuka attempted his Superfly Splash from the top of a steel cage, but Backlund rolled out of the way in time, causing Snuka's spectacular maneuver to backfire and cost him the match.

By 1983, World Wrestling Federation had been purchased by Vincent K. McMahon, who had a very different approach from his more traditional father. McMahon wanted a larger-than-life flashy Superstar as the standard-bearer of his organization, and it was clear that "The All-American Boy" would not fit the bill. Backlund's days were numbered.

"There was no denying his talent," remembered Freddie Blassie in his autobiography, *Listen, You Pencil Neck Geeks*. "But he didn't have the same pizzazz as, say, an Iron Sheik or Roddy Piper. There were big changes ahead, and unfortunately, they didn't seem to involve Backlund."

It was the Iron Sheik, one of Blassie's protégés, who brought the Backlund era to a close on December 26, 1983, in one of the most controversial matches in WWE history. With Backlund trapped in the Sheik's dreaded camel clutch submission hold yet unwilling to surrender, his manager Skaaland literally threw in the towel for his man, causing referee Dick Kroll to award the submission victory and the championship to the Iron Sheik.

"I don't think I was ever really over [popular] with the people," admits Backlund. "I was over with Vince Sr., and he wanted me to be the champion. His son took over and made a business decision. It was a decision that broke my heart, but I can't say it was the wrong decision. He made millions of dollars with that decision."

Just like that, it was all over, and Backlund disappeared from World Wrestling Federation, as well as the sport, very shortly afterward. For years, fans wondered if they'd ever again see the once-proud titleholder who had fallen victim to changing times.

In 1992, nearly nine years later, Backlund ended the speculation by launching a comeback in World Wrestling Federation. But his no-nonsense, no-gimmick approach was very out of place in the 1990s, and Backlund realized at last that a change was needed. In the summer of 1994, after failing in his attempt to regain the Heavyweight Championship from Bret "Hit Man" Hart, he snapped, attacking Hart after the match and showing a maniacal side of himself that had never been seen before.

Referring to himself as "Mr. Bob Backlund," he transformed into an ultra-right-wing conservative, delivering self-righteous rants filled with five-dollar words and condemning modern-day sports entertainment and its fans every chance he got. He also took to slapping his unbreakable cross-face chicken wing on as many unsuspecting victims as he could get his hands on.

Backlund's antics definitely got him more attention. At the *Survivor Series 1994*, he challenged Hart again in a Towel match, and this time was successful in taking back the Heavyweight crown—albeit in a fashion just as controversial as the manner in which he lost it. Eleven years after losing the title, Backlund had regained it—the longest such gap in wrestling history. But he didn't have long to savor it, because just three days later, in Madison Square Garden, he was defeated in a record eight seconds by Kevin Nash (then known as Diesel).

Following the loss, Backlund's career began to wind down. In 1996, he announced that he would run for president, but was unsuccessful in his bid. His last hurrah came in 1997, when he ironically joined up with the Iron Sheik to manage the masked Sultan (now known as Rikishi).

The last throwback to a bygone era, Bob Backlund was out of place from the start in the bizarre, larger-than-life WWE. Neither the company nor its fans had ever really gone in for such strait-laced, down-to-earth types, but despite it all, Backlund managed to carve out an unforgettable legacy for himself. In the end, he gave in to the overwhelming current of change, but his fans will always remember the "All-American Boy."

- In January 1992, Snuka faced Shawn Michaels in his first solo appearance at Madison Square Garden.

- Snuka was at one time married to The Rock's aunt.

- Snuka's popular "I Love You" hand gesture was incorporated into hip-hop culture in the early 1980s.

Few Superstars can be said to have single-handedly influenced the development of sports entertainment, but Jimmy Snuka is one of them. His innovative high-flying style was the precursor to much of what fans see each week on *Raw* and *SmackDown!* from the likes of Rob Van Dam and Rey Mysterio. The man who popularized maneuvers from the top rope, he was at one time the most popular competitor on the roster.

Snuka was born James Reiher on May 18, 1943, in the South Pacific island nation of Fiji. He showed an early interest in baseball and was an excellent hitter and outfielder. But any hopes of a professional career were dashed by the fact that he could not wear cleats without intense discomfort, having grown accustomed to going barefoot all his life in Fiji.

JIMMY "SUPERFLY" SNUKA

HEIGHT: 6'

WEIGHT: 250 lbs.

FROM: The Fiji Islands

YEARS IN WWE: 1982–85; 1989–92

CAREER HIGHLIGHTS: NWA U.S. Champion (1978-79); 2-time NWA World Tag Team Champion (1978–79, w/ Paul Orndorff; 1980, w/ Ray Stevens); 1996 WWE Hall of Famer

FINISHING MANEUVER: Superfly Splash

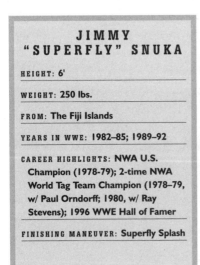

He decided to enter a sport where he could be allowed to compete barefoot, and began his wrestling career in Hawaii in 1969 under the name Jimmy Kealoha. By the beginning of the 1970s, he had made his way to North America, where he would spend the rest of his career.

While competing in the NWA's Pacific Northwest (PNW) territory in the early 1970s, he changed his ring name to Jimmy Snuka. He also held the PNW Tag Team Championship on seven occasions, six of them with local legend Dutch Savage. Between 1973 and 1977, he held the Pacific Northwest Heavyweight title six times, defeating such individuals as Bull Ramos and Jesse "The Body" Ventura.

"I first met Jimmy Snuka out in Portland, Oregon," remembers Sgt. Slaughter. "It was my second year in professional wrestling, and he was like a god out there. What I remember mostly was that he was a really good family man. He had two or three children already at that time. All of his extra time would either be spent at home or at the gym."

He also spent some time in the Vancouver territory, where he held the Canadian Tag Team title with Don Leo Jonathan in 1976, and in Dallas's World Class Championship Wrestling (WCCW), where he was Texas Champion in 1977.

He would spend the next few years competing in the Mid-Atlantic area, at that time the heart of the NWA. He teamed with fellow future WWE Superstar Paul Orndorff to win the NWA World Tag Team Championship in December 1978. Ten months later, he was victorious over another future WWE Superstar, Ricky Steamboat, in the finals of a U.S. Championship tournament.

Insisting on wrestling barefoot, as many of his Pacific Islander brethren did, Snuka was a sight to see, and his stint in Mid-Atlantic was the beginning of his meteoric rise. By that time, he had taken to referring to himself as "Superfly," in reference to his incredible aerial style of wrestling. Most notable of all was the leap off the top turnbuckle that he had perfected. Now a commonplace maneuver, back then it was unique, and led to countless wins for Snuka.

The Superfly continued to indulge his love for baseball by

competing in charity games whenever he could—barefoot, of course.

"It was like watching a deer when he would hit the ball and run," says Slaughter. "He'd hit a ball to third base and would beat the throw to first not by inches, but by feet! When he hit the ball, it hurt your ears, it echoed so much off the bat. He was such a wonderful athlete, even beyond wrestling."

After losing the U.S. title to Ric Flair, Snuka's second NWA World Tag Team title reign came with Ray "The Crippler" Stevens in June 1980. When this run was ended by Paul Jones & the Masked Superstar five months later, the Superfly finally departed Mid-Atlantic and headed to another NWA stronghold, Georgia Championship Wrestling (GCW). There, he joined forces with Terry "Bam Bam" Gordy, a founding member of the Fabulous Freebirds, to win the NWA National Tag Team Championship.

But bigger things were on the horizon. In 1982, Snuka made his World Wrestling Federation debut under the management of Capt. Lou Albano. Instantly rocketing to the top of contention, he challenged Heavyweight Champion Bob Backlund in three consecutive main events at Madison Square Garden, culminating in a historic Steel Cage match on June 28, 1982, in which he leapt from the top of the fifteen-foot cage, only to miss his opponent and consequently lose the match.

Later in the year, the course of Snuka's career was altered when he discovered, thanks to the legendary Buddy Rogers (then working as an announcer), that his manager Albano was ripping him off. Snuka fired Albano and hired Rogers as his new representation, winning the fans over in the process. He was the target of a bloody attack by Albano and his new charge Ray Stevens, which led to one of the early 1980s' most violent rivalries.

The following year, Snuka pursued Don Muraco's Intercontinental Championship. Their war was highlighted by another MSG Steel Cage match. This time, Snuka hit with his leap off the top of the cage, but it was unfortunately after he had already lost the match. By this time, Snuka was hands-down the most popular Superstar in the company.

"Snuka had a hard time expressing himself verbally," explains Slaughter. "Whatever the reason, it may have been the lights or the cameras, but that's the way he was. But he definitely loved his fans, and they loved him back."

The main way the Superfly expressed that was through his famous "I love you" hand gesture, which was always returned by his adoring fans.

"In June 1983, I attended my first match at Madison Square Garden," wrote Mick Foley—a rabid Snuka fan—in his 1999 autobiography, *Have a Nice Day!* "To see Jimmy Snuka battle Don Muraco in a bloody double disqualification. I was hooked. . . . The magic in the air was unmistakable [the night of their Steel Cage match]. I saw Snuka's unmistakable display of rage inside the ring. When it came to displays of rage, no one was more animated than Snuka. [He] climbed to the top rope, and the Garden stood in unison. We were about to see the famed Superfly leap. After all these years, it's still the most impressive sight I've ever seen—the muscular Snuka standing barefoot on top of the cage, his face a mask of crimson, while flashbulbs bathed him in light. It was a defining moment in my life—it was the day I knew without a doubt what I wanted to do with my life."

Next came "Rowdy" Roddy Piper, who drew the ire of the Superfly by smashing a coconut on his head during a segment of *Piper's Pit* in January 1984. After settling up with the Rowdy Scot, Snuka made an appearance at the first *WrestleMania*, where he was the corner man for Hulk Hogan & Mr. T in the main event.

Not long after, Snuka disappeared from the scene, just as the company was going national. He missed out on much of the glory days of the 1980s, but made a return to action in 1989 at *Wrestle-Mania V*. He was no longer the Superfly of old, but still enjoyed a few more years in the spotlight, including a match with the rookie Undertaker in 1991 at *WrestleMania VII*.

The Superfly still competes to this day. He's spent the majority of the past decades appearing on the Northeast independent circuit. In 1992, he became the very first ECW Heavyweight Champion, beating Salvatore Bellomo in a tournament final. Proving that some things never change, he lost that title to none other than Don Muraco. He made his final wrestling appearance in WWE to date at the *Survivor Series 1996*, where he returned to the Garden to take to the air once again. More recently, he's appeared on *Raw* on several occasions, and his ovations prove that the Superfly is far from forgotten.

- Among those Sarge brought to WWE in his capacity as talent scout: Razor Ramon, the Smoking Gunns, the 1-2-3 Kid, Yokozuna, Undertaker, and Diesel.

- In the early 1980s, Slaughter was asked by the U.S. Department of the Navy to cease associating himself on TV with the Marine Corps.

- Sarge's camouflage limo, the Slaughtermobile, was once permanently housed in the parking lot of WWE's Stamford headquarters, Titan Tower.

In the lexicon of popular culture, only a handful of pro wrestlers have ever been able to really penetrate to mainstream status. Yet thanks to one of the most charismatic and memorable personas ever devised, Sgt. Slaughter is one of them. Perhaps no other Superstar with his level of name recognition enjoyed such equal notoriety as both a hated villain and a lauded hero. Whether as an American icon, an Iraqi sympathizer, or even a cartoon character, the Sarge always made an impression.

He was born Robert Remus on August 27, 1948, in Buford,

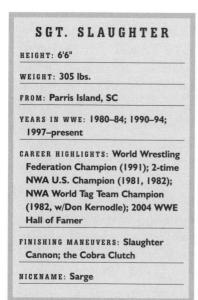

SGT. SLAUGHTER

HEIGHT: 6'6"

WEIGHT: 305 lbs.

FROM: Parris Island, SC

YEARS IN WWE: 1980–84; 1990–94; 1997–present

CAREER HIGHLIGHTS: World Wrestling Federation Champion (1991); 2-time NWA U.S. Champion (1981, 1982); NWA World Tag Team Champion (1982, w/Don Kernodle); 2004 WWE Hall of Famer

FINISHING MANEUVERS: Slaughter Cannon; the Cobra Clutch

NICKNAME: Sarge

South Carolina, but spent much of his early life in Litchfield, Minnesota, on the military base where his father was stationed. As a young man, he joined the Marine Corps, where he earned the moniker that would later become a household name. After serving out his time in the Corps, Remus turned to professional wrestling as a part-time career. Having grown up on the action of the midwestern-based American Wrestling Association (AWA), he was already an avid fan of the sport.

After his 1974 debut in the Pacific Northwest, among his earliest incarnations were Big Bob Slaughter and Bruiser Bob Slaughter. When his mother was stricken with cancer, Bob took a break from the business and went back home to run his father's roofing company so his father could spend all his time with her. It was during this time away that he came up with just what he needed to make it in the sport he had left.

"One day, we couldn't do any work because it was raining. I was watching a movie on TV called *The D.I.* with Jack Webb," he remembers. "I just got this thought in my mind: Why hasn't anyone brought a drill instructor character like this into professional wrestling? No one ever was a drill instructor. I dug out my old campaign cover and my fatigues. Of course, nothing fit at that time, but the idea was there."

The name would be derived from that nickname his fellow marines had once attached to him: Sgt. Slaughter. Inspired by the Webb character, Sarge would be an antagonistic, abrasive, bullying drill instructor. In 1976, he brought the idea to AWA promoter Verne Gagne in Minnesota. Gagne was intrigued, remembering how much he had hated his own drill instructor.

Sgt. Slaughter first appeared in the Central States promotion of Bob Geigel, a territory affiliated at the time with the AWA. Clad in full drill instructor regalia, with fatigues, hat, sunglasses, and whistle, the Sarge was quite an imposing figure. In his gruff, booming voice, he would criticize both fans and opponents alike as if they were his newest recruits. The fans ate it up. They hated him right from the get-go.

But before Sgt. Slaughter could really take off in the AWA as had been planned, Sarge struck up a fateful friendship.

"I got to know Pat Patterson quite well, and started telling him about the Slaughter character that I had already been successful with," says Sarge. "Pat said he was going to New York City to start working for Vince McMahon Sr. and suggested that I give him some photos and things to take with him. I did, and shortly after that I got a call from Vince McMahon Sr. He thought it was quite a clever character and wanted me to come in."

And so Sgt. Slaughter was debuted in World Wrestling Federation in 1980. His first appearance was a speech delivered at one of the Federation's TV tapings in Allentown, Pennsylvania, after three hours of taping.

"Mr. McMahon came in and said, 'Are you ready?' I said sure. He said, 'Can I set up anything for you?' I said, 'Yes, here's a tape of the Marine Corps Hymn, would you play that when I go out?' He said, 'Music . . . That's never been done here. Let's try it.' I came out with all my gear on, and before I got to the microphone people wanted to come over the railing and get me, because I was really into the character and was a bad guy. I finally did the promo, and we almost had a riot, which was pretty incredible since no one knew me or had ever seen me there up to this point, and the audience had been pretty worn down from watching three hours of wrestling. When I went to the back, all the boys in the locker room stood in awe. Vince Sr. came over and shook my hand and said, 'That's the greatest thing I've ever seen in this business, when can you start?' "

The Sarge was immediately placed in the main event at Madison Square Garden against Heavyweight Champion Bob Backlund. Few Superstars had ever risen to main event status so quickly.

Slaughter appeared at the next Garden date in a match against Bruno Sammartino, which turned out to be Sammartino's last MSG appearance before his retirement. Several months later Sarge wound up in a feud with Patterson that finished with the famous Alley Fight at Madison Square Garden, one of the most brutal and bloody matches in WWE history. The Sarge was on a roll, and remained one of the company's top villains for years, even while stepping out from time to time to compete elsewhere.

Sgt. Slaughter vs. Pat Patterson.

During these absences, Slaughter spent considerable time in the NWA's Mid-Atlantic territory, winning the U.S. title twice in the early 1980s, from Ricky Steamboat and Wahoo McDaniel. He also teamed with Don Kernodle to take the World Tag Team title from the Minnesota Wrecking Crew in a Tag Team tournament in Japan.

Sarge took another shot at Backlund in 1983, but a few months later something amazing happened. After coming face-to-face with America-bashing villains like the Iron Sheik and Mr. Fuji, Slaughter found that his red, white, and blue image was attracting cheers from the crowd. With *Hulkamania* taking off in 1984, Sgt. Slaughter was reborn as one of the Federation's superheroes, rivaling the Hulkster in popularity.

His war with the Iron Sheik over the summer of 1984 is the stuff of legend. The two met on three consecutive occasions at MSG, as well as at nearly all the other venues, major and minor, throughout the ever-growing Federation circuit. It was a classic battle of the all-American patriot against the embodiment of all that America feared and hated. Their matches headlined arenas in one part of the country, while Hogan headlined in another part.

"We really had it going on," Slaughter says. "Hogan sold out the West, I sold out the East. Then, Hogan would sell out the East and I'd sell out the West. We were a powerhouse."

But an unexpected occurrence took place in late 1984 that would cause Slaughter to walk out of the Federation just as it was experiencing a national explosion. He was asked by Hasbro Toys, the manufacturers of G.I. Joe, to become the spokesman for the company's line of action figures and cartoons. Looking to capitalize on his patriotic image, they even wanted to give Sarge his own figure and make him a character on the show, the first and only living character in the thirty-year history of G.I. Joe. But Slaughter and Vince McMahon didn't see eye to eye on the matter, and it became an issue of choosing between the Federation and G.I. Joe. Sarge chose the latter.

For five years, Sgt. Slaughter was associated with G.I. Joe, maintaining a high profile even though his association with the wrestling business was minimal. During that time, most of his time in the ring was spent working in the AWA.

"In 1990, I got a call from Vince on a Sunday afternoon," he remembers. "I was just kinda dozing off, watching a NASCAR race on TV, when the phone rang. I said, 'Hello?' A voice said 'Sarge, it's Vince.' There's only one Vince. He said, 'Do you feel like going back to work?' and I said, 'I sure do.' "

And so Slaughter returned to World Wrestling Federation. But instead of taking advantage of the G.I. Joe exposure, the character went in a totally different direction. Sarge returned to his villainous roots, becoming an Iraqi sympathizer during a time when the

United States was on the brink of war with Saddam Hussein for the first time.

With Hussein lookalike General Adnan by his side, Slaughter once again drew the hatred of Federation fans. To make matters worse, he captured the Heavyweight Championship from the Ultimate Warrior at the *Royal Rumble 1991*. This led to a confrontation with Hulk Hogan at *WrestleMania VII*, in which matters were set right when the "American-Made" Hulkster toppled Sarge to regain the title.

After losing his gold, Slaughter made an about-face, declaring, "I want my country back!" and begging fans to take him back into their good graces. The fans obliged, and Slaughter went out as one of the good guys. He retired from full-time competition in 1992 and became a talent scout for the company. He filled this role for two more years before parting ways with the Federation.

But in 1997, during the Federation's war with WCW, Vince brought Sarge back for a run that continues to this day. At first, he played the part of the Federation's first commissioner, filling in for ailing president Gorilla Monsoon. As such, he was one of Vince McMahon's "stooges" during the chairman's memorable late-1990s rivalry with Stone Cold Steve Austin. But when that situation blew over and the commissionership passed from his hands to Shawn Michaels, there was still a place for Sarge behind the scenes.

Sarge became a trusted road agent, imparting his wisdom to the active Superstars and helping to run events from backstage. Now and then, he's been known to break out the fatigues and hit the ring, like when he opposed Triple H at *In Your House: D-Generation X* or competed in the Gimmick Battle Royal at *WrestleMania X-Seven*. In 2003, he had a match with up-and-coming Superstar and future World Heavyweight Champion Randy Orton.

"That was a real thrill for me," Sarge says, "because I had wrestled Randy's grandfather [Cowboy Bob Orton Sr.], his father [Cowboy Bob Orton Jr.], and his uncle [Barry Orton]."

One of WWE's truly enduring figures, Sgt. Slaughter is a living bridge between the era of legends and the present day.

DIRTY ROTTEN SCOUNDRELS:

THE FOLKS YOU LOVED TO HATE

- Legendary country music singer Hank Williams once proposed to Moolah, and was turned down!

- Moolah was good friends with both Elvis Presley and Jerry Lee Lewis, who often attended her matches in the 1950s.

- Moolah came back for another match in 2003—after turning eighty.

In the world of women's wrestling, there will always be one irrefutable legend that stands head and shoulders above the rest: the Fabulous Moolah. She was the longest-reigning champion in the history of her chosen sport, or any sport for that matter. With more than fifty years in the business to her credit, she has established a legacy that will never be forgotten, making her name synonymous with female wrestling.

Born Lillian Ellison in 1923, she was trained for the ring in the 1940s by then–Women's Championship Mildred Burke, the sport's biggest female star at the time. But her career actually began outside the ring, where she served as one of wrestling's first female valets. Dubbed "Slave Girl Moolah" by promoter Jack Pfefer, she was an alluring presence at ringside for competitors such as the

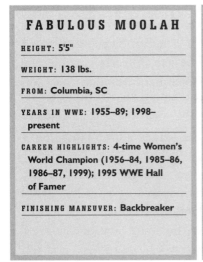

FABULOUS MOOLAH

HEIGHT: 5'5"

WEIGHT: 138 lbs.

FROM: Columbia, SC

YEARS IN WWE: 1955–89; 1998–present

CAREER HIGHLIGHTS: 4-time Women's World Champion (1956–84, 1985–86, 1986–87, 1999); 1995 WWE Hall of Famer

FINISHING MANEUVER: Backbreaker

gruesome Elephant Boy and the U.S. Champion "Nature Boy" Buddy Rogers.

Her in-ring career began hitting its stride by the mid-1950s, when she began calling herself the "Fabulous Moolah." In 1956, she defeated Judy Grable in a tournament final for the vacant Women's Championship of the World. She would go on to hold the title for the next twenty-eight years, a feat unprecedented in the annals of sports history.

"I'll tell ya one thing straight out, darlin'," she wrote in her 2002 autobiography, *First Goddess of the Squared Circle*. "Ain't nothing like being the best in the world at what you do. And that's what I was. I don't say this to brag or to sound conceited, I say it 'cause it's a plain and simple fact now as I look back on it. . . . Once I got that championship, I didn't stop working. If anything, I worked harder, because I knew the girls would be gunning for me. My goal was not just to become the champion, but to stay at the top. That's what Mildred Burke did, and I wanted to dominate just like she had done."

Recognized by the National Wrestling Alliance (NWA), Moolah traveled throughout the nation defending her title on a regular basis in all the NWA's member territories, including the fledgling World Wide Wrestling Federation, which was then based in the northeastern United States. During that time, there were several occasions where it appeared that she had been defeated for her title (against Betty Boucher in 1966, Yukiko Tomoe in 1968, and Sue Green in 1976). However, she remained recognized by the majority of promoters for an uninterrupted period of time from the 1950s all the way to the 1980s. One of the greatest achievements of this period came in 1972, when she and Vincent J. McMahon successfully beat the ban against women's wrestling at Madison Square Garden.

By 1983, Moolah signed a deal with new World Wrestling Frederation owner Vincent K. McMahon to compete exclusively for him, and her Women's Championship became a critical part of the company's national expansion. Ironically enough, only a few months later, in July 1984, her twenty-eight-year reign was ended in Madison Square Garden by Wendi Richter, a young competitor managed by pop star Cyndi Lauper who was at the time the female equivalent of Hulk Hogan.

"I was heartbroken for a while at losing my championship," wrote Moolah. "I knew everybody was right when they said I had had an amazing run, but it still hurt."

Moolah began phasing out her in-ring exploits, choosing instead to manage Hawaiian Superstar Leilani Kai. With Moolah's guidance, Kai beat Richter for the Women's title, setting up a match between the two at the first *WrestleMania* in 1985. Richter would regain the gold, and it would be Moolah herself, under a mask as the "Spider Lady," who would finally take back the Championship from Wendi not long after.

After trading the title back and forth with Australian grappler Velvet McIntyre, she returned from a tour Down Under with her gold intact. It would be while competing in Houston that Moolah was conclusively parted from her title once and for all, when she was beaten in 1987 by "Sensational" Sherri Martel. Following the loss, Moolah became less and less a part of the wrestling scene, until she completely disappeared. It seemed that the queen of women's wrestling had finally come to the end of her run.

Imagine the surprise of fans everywhere when in 1999, Moolah—by that time in her seventies—returned to television, this time with longtime friend and fellow competitor Mae Young by her side. Then in October, at *No Mercy '99*, the unthinkable happened: Moolah defeated reigning Women's Championship Ivory to win the title for the fourth time and become the oldest titleholder in the history of the sport.

"It felt right, like a baby being returned to its mama," she wrote. "I kept thinking, *I'm the champ again—in my seventies!* I thought of all the wacky characters I knew and loved and battled during a lifetime in this crazy business, and a lump formed in my throat. I'd just done something nobody had ever done."

She didn't hold the title long, but it was a testament to her amazing tenacity and ability that she was able to make such a miraculous comeback in the first place. She and Mae Young continue to be a part of the extended WWE family to this day. In 2004, she was featured prominently in the documentary film *Lipstick and Dynamite,* which chronicles the golden age of women's wrestling. She maintains a wrestling school for women, imparting her years of priceless wisdom to a new generation of athletes.

- There was once an underground New York City punk band named Killer Kowalski in honor of the wrestler.
- Killer Kowalski is a strict vegetarian.

Very few performers in the history of the business have names that are instantly recognizable to almost anyone, regardless of whether they are wrestling fans or not. But Killer Kowalski is one of the select few. His name has entered the popular imagination, even if many people who know the name may not know about the man it's attached to—the man whose fearsome demeanor and brutal ring tactics made him one of the sport's top villains and main-eventers for three decades.

Wladek Kowalski was born October 13, 1926, in Windsor, Ontario, Canada, the son of Polish immigrants. The family later moved to Detroit, Michigan, where Wladek's father got work in an automobile factory. As a young man in the 1940s, Wladek—whose name was Americanized to Walter—joined his father in the factory for a short time. But he was restless, and yearned for something different than the nine-to-five assembly-line routine.

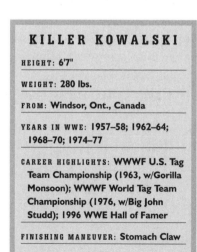

KILLER KOWALSKI

HEIGHT: 6'7"

WEIGHT: 280 lbs.

FROM: Windsor, Ont., Canada

YEARS IN WWE: 1957–58; 1962–64; 1968–70; 1974–77

CAREER HIGHLIGHTS: WWWF U.S. Tag Team Championship (1963, w/Gorilla Monsoon); WWWF World Tag Team Championship (1976, w/Big John Studd); 1996 WWE Hall of Famer

FINISHING MANEUVER: Stomach Claw

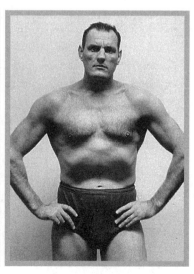

At twenty, he decided to take advantage of his impressive size to break into professional wrestling, a business that—thanks to the advent of television—was in the midst of a dramatic renaissance and seemed like a great way to make a living, and then some. In 1947, he made his ring debut under the name Tarzan Kowalski, a tall, youthful rookie who was deemed a natural babyface, or fan favorite.

Kowalski made his first splash in Morris Seigel's Houston, Texas, promotion, which was part of the National Wrestling Alliance. In August 1950, in one of several historic matches with "Nature Boy" Buddy Rogers, he defeated Rogers for his first title, the NWA Texas Heavyweight Championship. Later that year, he beat Texas Tag Team Champions Duke Keomuka & Danny Savich in a Handicap match, and claimed the newly created title by himself.

Slowly but surely, Kowalski built up a reputation in territory after territory. In San Francisco, he captured the Pacific Coast Tag Team title in 1951 with the equally immense Hans Hermann. Later that year in Kansas City, he won the NWA Central States Championship, upending Wild Bill Longson, legendary World Champion of the 1940s.

But it was in Eddie Quinn's Montreal promotion that the Kowalski legend began to take flight. On January 14, 1953, he took part in the first wrestling match ever televised in Canada, facing Yukon Eric in the Montreal Forum. One year later, he was rematched against Eric at the Forum, leading to an infamous incident that is talked about to this day: administering his patented flying kneedrop, Kowalski came down on Yukon Eric's head, tearing off his ear.

"I came off the ropes and grazed his cheek with my shin," remembered Kowalski. "I caught his cauliflower ear, and part of it ripped off and rolled across the ring. It was still throbbing when the referee picked it up. Eddie Quinn demanded that I go to Yukon Eric's hospital room and apologize. I never apologized for these things in my life. They happen. But when I got there, I saw all the bandages around his face and I thought, 'Humpty Dumpty sat on the wall. Humpty Dumpty had a great fall.' I started laughing, and when the Montreal press found out about it, I became the most hated man in wrestling."

Whether he liked it or not, "Tarzan" Kowalski's run as a strapping fan favorite was over. Killer Kowalski was born. Wrestling fans nationwide got wind of the incident, and Kowalski's reputation was set for life. He became one of the industry's top-drawing stars, transcending territorial boundaries. As much as with his actions, he struck fear in the hearts of opponents and fans with his terrifying interviews.

"I developed my interview style while driving," he says. "No one wanted to travel with me. I guess I'm not that much fun to be around. No beer drinking or smoking was ever allowed in my car. So I'd listen to the radio and create imaginary arguments with the commentators."

For a decade, his main base of operations was Montreal, where on eleven occasions he won that promotion's version of the World Heavyweight title (which had splintered from the widely established version of the World title in 1937). The impressive list of those he defeated for the crown include Bobby Managoff, Verne Gagne, Yvon Robert, Antonino Rocca, Pat O'Connor, Don Leo Jonathan, Hard Boiled Haggerty, Buddy Rogers, and Johnny Rougeau.

In 1957, Killer Kowalski ventured to the Northeast for the first time to work for Vincent J. McMahon, whose Capitol Wrestling Corporation was in the process of becoming the dominant promotion in that part of the nation. He debuted at the old Madison Square Garden, teaming with Dick the Bruiser to challenge U.S. Tag Team Champions Antonino Rocca & Miguel Perez.

Kowalski returned to the Northeast in 1962, at a time when McMahon's territory was on the verge of breaking away from the NWA to become World Wide Wrestling Federation. In October 1962 and January 1963, he challenged NWA World Champion Buddy Rogers in Madison Square Garden. The match took place just three days before Rogers lost the title to Lou Thesz, and was the last time the NWA World title would be defended in the Garden prior to the creation of the independent WWWF.

In August 1963, Kowalski challenged the new WWWF Heavyweight Champion Bruno Sammartino for the first of what would be many times. Over the years, the Killer would go on to be one of Sammartino's longest-standing and best-remembered foes.

That fall, one of the most fearsome duos in WWE history was formed, as two of the company's most hated Superstars, Kowalski and Gorilla Monsoon, joined forces. In November, they beat Skull Murphy & Brute Bernard for the U.S. Tag Team Championship in Washington, D.C., and they held the belts for a month and a half before losing them to the Tolos Brothers in Teaneck, New Jersey. The duo remained together for several more months, making life difficult for WWWF's heroes until Kowalski departed in 1964.

He returned to WWWF in 1968 and made an even more serious run at the still-reigning Sammartino. He steamrolled over Bruno's "cousin" Antonio Pugliese, and reunited with Gorilla Monsoon to make a two-pronged assault. He opposed Bruno in two straight main events at MSG, with neither resulting in a clear winner. Then, in mid-1969, Kowalski lost his Tag Team partner when Gorilla Monsoon formed an alliance with Sammartino to become one of WWWF's most popular Superstars, leading to a bitter feud between the two former comrades.

During another of his national tours, Kowalski went to work for Fritz Von Erich's fledgling World Class Championship Wrestling in Dallas. Another major stop was the high-profile Los Angeles territory, where he won the prestigious NWA Americas Championship in 1972. He also enjoyed a brief reign as NWA Americas Tag Team Champions with Kenji Shibuya later that year.

By now a grizzled veteran approaching the age of fifty, in 1974 Kowalski headed back to the WWWF for one last run to finish out his career. He once again challenged Heavyweight Champion Sammartino in back-to-back Garden main events, this time finally losing to him in the second encounter, a Texas Death match. He also feuded extensively with both Pedro Morales and Andre the Giant.

In the final years of his career, Kowalski became a wrestling trainer. One of his earliest prospects was John Minton, who would

later gain renown as Big John Studd. Wishing for Minton to get experience without being overshadowed by him, he Tag Teamed with his young student in WWWF as the masked Executioners. Their identities hidden, Kowalski & Minton dethroned Tony Parisi (Antonio Pugliese) & Louis Cerdan to win the World Tag Team title in May 1976. They held the gold until October, when WWWF officials stripped them for allowing a third masked member (Nikolai Volkoff) to defend the title.

After calling it quits in 1977, Kowalski focused completely on his work as a trainer, opening up the Killer Kowalski School of Professional Wrestling in Salem, Massachusetts (relocating to Malden in 1987). There, he redirected all the fire and passion he had for the sport into preparing a new generation of athletes. Among his many graduates are Luna Vachon, Perry Saturn, Chyna, A-Train, and undoubtedly his greatest pupil of all, Triple H.

"He took a liking to me, partially I think because I'm Polish," says Kowalski's most recent Superstar alumnus, Chris Nowinski.

"When you meet the Killer, he just seems like a wise prophet in some ways. He loves to sit down with you and give you advice on your life, on wrestling, share stories and experiences. He has a very unique perspective on existence. Knowing how much of a legend he is, it was great that he'd always sit down and share his experiences with the new guys. Never let him drop that knee on you, though!"

- Valentine was known for his practical jokes or "ribs," which could often be cruel or disgusting to the extreme.
- Chess, fine wines, and classical music were among the eccentric Valentine's interests.
- Lou Thesz called Johnny Valentine "The toughest and most courageous performer I ever saw."

A legend for his ruggedness and ring psychology, Johnny Valentine was both a major draw and a major influence, that rare individual who is revered by his colleagues as much as by the fans. He was a headliner during Capitol Wrestling's early years in the late 1950s and early '60s, but also traveled to countless other territories, collecting championships everywhere he went. Despite the tragic accident that cut his career short in 1975, Valentine had more than enough time to make a major impact on the sport.

He was born John Theodore Wisniski on September 22, 1928, in Hobart, Washington, a logging town outside Seattle. As a youth, he trained to be a boxer, but was discovered by a local wrestling promoter in 1947 at age nineteen and began his grappling career.

JOHNNY VALENTINE

HEIGHT: 6'4"

WEIGHT: 255 lbs.

FROM: Seattle, WA

YEARS IN WWE: 1958–62; 1965–66

CAREER HIGHLIGHTS: 4-time U.S. Tag Team Champion (1959–60, w/Dr. Jerry Graham; 1960, w/Buddy Rogers; 1962, w/Cowboy Bob Ellis; 1966, w/Antonio Pugliese)

FINISHING MANEUVER: Brainbuster

NICKNAME: Handsome Johnny

He got his first taste for the rough side of the business when he was stranded in South America by one promoter and was forced to literally work his way back, making money by wrestling along the way. Perhaps this is one of the experiences that contributed to making him the often cold, inscrutable personality he eventually became.

From the beginning, he was a traveler, making his name in territory after territory and then moving on: Florida, Texas, Minnesota, among others. He bleached his hair blond to take advantage of the popular fad sweeping the wrestling game at the time. But that wasn't the only thing that got him attention. Unlike the other blond pretty boys, Valentine was tough as nails, understated yet menacing on his interviews, vicious and brutal in the ring. This came across to fans, who instinctively respected him, even as they booed him.

Despite his lack of wrestling technique, he was such a rough brawler that even the so-called legit mat wrestlers feared him. Among the stories from those days is the one in which Valentine went head-to-head with a bull at a local rodeo, stunning the beast with a punch to the face that allowed him to escape over the fence. Whether accurate or not, such tales tend only to accumulate around a kernel of truth.

In the summer of 1958, he made his way to Capitol Wrestling in the Northeast for the first time, wrestling for Vincent J. McMahon. At first, he was a straight-up ring villain, winning the U.S. Tag Team title with such notorious rogues as Dr. Jerry Graham and Buddy Rogers. But much as Stone Cold Steve Austin would do forty years later, Valentine slowly won over audiences with his confident, aggressive, no-nonsense style.

"He was a great performer," says Ric Flair, who spent a lot of time around Valentine during the latter years of his career in the Carolinas during the 1970s. "If a promoter had a lot of patience, his style worked very well. He was strictly a wrestler, and liked using holds for long periods of time. Sometimes it was hard for the crowd to get into it at first, but once he won them over, he was gangbusters. People really believed he was that tough, and he was."

Johnny Valentine vs. Buddy Rogers.

By the end of 1960, he was a full-fledged fan favorite, embroiled in a tumultuous war with U.S. Champion—and former ally—Buddy Rogers. As a draw, he was extremely valuable, taking part in a series of main events at Madison Square Garden that is among the longest sellout streaks in Garden history.

When he returned to the newly renamed World Wide Wrestling Federation in 1965, however, it didn't take him long to return to his old ways. He turned on his last Tag Team championship partner, Antonio Pugliese, abandoning him and the title in the middle of a match. It was far from a stretch for the man who, despite being among the most respected competitors, was never among the most

liked. Part of that had to do with his often-sadistic penchant for ribbing, or playing practical jokes.

"We all enjoyed a good practical joke, but Valentine took it to
the extreme," wrote "Classy" Freddie Blassie in his 2003 autobiography. One of the most extreme and legendary Valentine ribs of all
time involved "The Alaskan" Jay York, an asthmatic wrestler who
needed to use his inhaler following every match. As legend has it,
one night Valentine secretly replaced the medication in the inhaler
with kerosene. Reportedly, York returned to the locker room the
next night with a sawed-off shotgun.

In the late 1960s, Valentine headed to the Houston-Dallas circuit, engaging in a rivalry with fellow tough guy Wahoo McDaniel
that many credit with reinvigorating business throughout Texas. In
the early 1970s, Valentine and McDaniel took their feud to the
Carolinas territory. At that time an area based around Tag Teams,
the Carolinas-based Jim Crockett Promotions was transformed in
part by Valentine's drawing power, soon becoming the flagship
promotion of the NWA (thirteen years later it transformed into
WCW).

On October 4, 1975, Valentine boarded a twin-engine Cessna
310 airplane from Charlotte to Wilmington, North Carolina, along
with several other Mid-Atlantic wrestlers and promoter David
Crockett. The plane ran out of fuel in mid-flight and crash-landed
one hundred feet from its runway destination. The pilot slipped
into a coma from which he never awoke. Rookie wrestler Ric Flair,
also onboard, suffered a broken back that put him on the shelf for
four months.

Valentine wasn't so lucky. His spine shattered by the impact,
he was rendered paralyzed from the waist down for the rest of his
life. At the time, he was NWA U.S. Champion and the top star in
the company. The man who would subsequently be groomed to
take that spot would be Flair, who had idolized Valentine and pat-
terned much of his style after his. Flair was just one of many young
performers who had studied Valentine's unique way of building
tension in a match, gradually drawing in the audience's attention
and never letting go.

Although Johnny Valentine never walked again, his name would remain alive in the business thanks to his son Greg "The Hammer" Valentine (John Wisniski Jr.), who achieved great fame in his own right in World Wrestling Federation during the 1980s.

In August 2000, Valentine suffered a fall from the porch of his home in the Fort Worth suburb of River Oaks, causing further back damage and internal injuries. His condition worsened, and though he fought hard for eight months, he never left the hospital, passing away on April 24, 2001, at age seventy-two. He was survived by his wife, Sharon, four children, five grandchildren, and one great-grandchild.

"I never gave up on the idea that I'd wrestle again," Valentine admitted to the *Dallas Morning News* in 1985. "The only time I ever really enjoyed life was my hour in the ring. There, I was king, you might say."

- Ladd briefly worked as a WWE announcer, and helped call the action at *WrestleMania 2*.

- Although he did not appear on TV, Ladd was on hand at the Fan Festival for *WrestleMania X-Seven* in Houston.

- At the end of his career, Ladd managed the Wild Samoans in Mid-South Wrestling.

Ernie Ladd has made a name for himself in several fields of endeavor. He was a dominating football player at both the college and pro level, and has been closely involved with the Republican Party for nearly thirty-five years. He was also one of the premiere professional wrestlers of the 1960s and 1970s. Longtime fans in the Northeast particularly remember the havoc he wreaked in the WWWF throughout the 1970s as one of the largest and most hated heels the territory had ever seen.

Ladd was born in the small town of Rayville, Louisiana, in November of 1938. His family moved to Texas when he was four years old, and the remainder of his upbringing took place in the Lone Star State. It was while attending high school in his home-

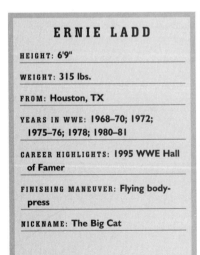

ERNIE LADD

HEIGHT: 6'9"

WEIGHT: 315 lbs.

FROM: Houston, TX

YEARS IN WWE: 1968–70; 1972; 1975–76; 1978; 1980–81

CAREER HIGHLIGHTS: 1995 WWE Hall of Famer

FINISHING MANEUVER: Flying body-press

NICKNAME: The Big Cat

town of Orange, Texas, that Ladd got his first taste of the gridiron when he caught the eye of one of the coaches (who happened to be the father of future football great Bubba Smith).

"I was a tall, rangy, skinny kid, and he just told me I had to come out for football," says Ladd. "I had no choice. In my school, we only had 400 kids from grade 1 to grade 12, and every kid who was big enough and had any coordination had to play football."

He was a star lineman for Louisiana's Grambling State University in the late 1950s, and was recruited in 1961 by the AFL's San Diego Chargers. He was a member of the Chargers' 1963 AFL championship team, and appeared in four straight AFL All-Star games from 1962 to 1965. In addition to the Chargers, he also played for the Houston Oilers and Kansas City Chiefs. At six-nine and over 300 pounds, Ladd was one of the largest players of his era, and his amazing quickness for his size earned him the nickname "Big Cat."

The wrestling world began to beckon Ladd in the early 1960s, while he was still a Charger. As a publicity stunt, some San Diego–area wrestlers challenged the Big Cat to a private workout session in the ring.

"I said, 'You guys aren't legit. I might hurt somebody.' So I went out there to hurt somebody, but they put me on the mat and stretched me. It became a great challenge to me because I couldn't wrestle, I was not in my arena. I wanted to learn."

The same wrestlers who had stretched him were more than happy to train him, and Ladd soon began wrestling for the Los Angeles promotion part-time during the football off-season. Due to his reputation as a pro ball player, Ladd quickly became one of wrestling's hottest draws, and was eagerly sought after by promoters across the nation. As if his mainstream name wasn't enough, Ladd also caught mat fans' attention by becoming one of the sport's most despised villains, often stirring up crowds with his cocky and color- ful interviews, and through the use of his infamous taped thumb (a gimmick Ladd now freely admits was stolen from "Crazy" Luke Graham). Ladd's heel status is particularly noteworthy because he was one of wrestling's first African-American villains during a time

when promoters feared such a character would provoke riots due to widespread racism.

By 1970, Ladd made the discovery that he could make more money as a wrestler than as a football player. He quit the AFL and went on the road as a full-time grappler.

He first appeared in World Wide Wrestling Federation in 1968. It would remain one of the main promotions in which he wrestled for the next twelve years. Managed by the Grand Wizard, he was a persistent challenger to Heavyweight Champions Bruno Sammartino, Pedro Morales, and Bob Backlund, although he never won the title. His feuds with fellow behemoths Andre the Giant, Haystacks Calhoun, and especially Gorilla Monsoon are the stuff of legend.

"Dominic DeNucci was was one of the greatest opponents I ever competed against," remembers Ladd. "We had a lot of fire, and there was a lot of electricity every time we met."

Ladd capped off his Federation career with a feud against up-and-comer Tony Atlas that culminated in a Texas Death match at Madison Square Garden in December 1980. He was inducted to the WWE Hall of Fame in 1995.

In addition to the Federation, the Big Cat also spent significant time in the Detroit territory and the World Wrestling Association (WWA), and was one of the top stars in the early days of Bill Watts's Mid-South Wrestling in the late 1970s. In 1981, Ladd finished his in-ring career in Dallas for World Class Championship Wrestling, battling the young Von Erich brothers.

"Age was catching up with me," he says. "You have to know when it's over. It had been good to me, but my back was going, my knees were bad. The old body was telling me, 'Time to find something else to do.'"

Ladd had no problem finding something else to do, because he had long been an active crusader for the Republican Party. Particularly, he's been a friend of the Bush family since the 1960s, and has campaigned for both George Bush and George W. Bush. At the beginning of 2001, George W. made Ladd a special deputy to his Presidential Inaugural Committee. In addition to his political activity, Ladd is part of a Christian ministry that travels to prisons and provides services to inmates.

The squared circle has played one of many parts in the multifaceted life of the Big Cat. But it's clear that that part holds a very special place in his heart.

"Wrestling's been a great passion in my life," he says. "It's always been good to me, and it's always been exciting to the fans. When you thrill the fans, it's enjoyable to me."

- Graham was one of the broadcasters for the first edition of *SummerSlam* in 1988.

- Graham both won the Heavyweight title with his feet on the ropes, and lost the Heavyweight title with his feet on the ropes.

- Graham, a consummate bodybuilder, met fellow enthusiast Arnold Schwarzenegger in the original Gold's Gym.

They say that there's nothing new under the sun, and when it comes to wrestling, there are few who have been able to come up with anything truly original. They're the ones who set the trends, and influence all those who follow. Superstar Billy Graham is one of those. Taking the flamboyant heel persona perfected by the likes of Gorgeous George and Buddy Rogers to a whole new level, he set the standard followed by men like Hulk Hogan and Jesse "The Body" Ventura.

He was born Eldridge Wayne Coleman in Phoenix, Arizona, on July 6, 1943. Taking a very early interest in bodybuilding, he was already weight training by the fifth grade, using makeshift

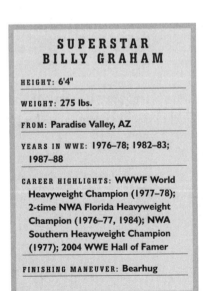

SUPERSTAR BILLY GRAHAM

HEIGHT: 6'4"

WEIGHT: 275 lbs.

FROM: Paradise Valley, AZ

YEARS IN WWE: 1976–78; 1982–83; 1987–88

CAREER HIGHLIGHTS: **WWWF World Heavyweight Champion (1977–78); 2-time NWA Florida Heavyweight Champion (1976–77, 1984); NWA Southern Heavyweight Champion (1977); 2004 WWE Hall of Famer**

FINISHING MANEUVER: **Bearhug**

weights made of cement. Religion was a part of his life from an early age as well, and Coleman even found a way to combine the two, appearing before congregations to preach and perform feats of strength by age eighteen.

In the late 1960s, Coleman was a part of the burgeoning body-building scene in California. It was in 1968, in Santa Monica, that he became acquainted with a young Austrian bodybuilder named Arnold Schwarzenegger, who had just arrived in the United States for the first time. The two became training partners and started a friendship that continues to this day.

Not long after, Coleman got the idea to enter the professional wrestling business. At the time, there was no one in the sport with anything resembling the chiseled, bodybuilder physique he possessed, and he knew such a look would be a novelty. In the winter of 1970, he headed north to Calgary to receive training in the infamous "Dungeon" of Stu Hart.

At first, he wrestled simply as Wayne Coleman, but that was about to change. "After I left Calgary and came back down to Phoenix, in the summer of '70, I was bouncing in a nightclub, and one day in walked Dr. Jerry Graham, the infamous wrestler who had actually been Vince McMahon's favorite when he was a kid. We started talking about wrestling, and I told him I was now an official wrestler after enduring Stu Hart's Dungeon. He suggested we start wrestling together."

They headed to Los Angeles as a Tag Team. Dr. Jerry had the idea to make Coleman into a member of the notorious Graham "family," which had previously included Eddie Graham and "Crazy" Luke Graham. Given his background, Coleman chose the name of evangelist Billy Graham, and later added Superstar as an homage to the rock opera *Jesus Christ Superstar*.

Superstar Billy Graham headed on his own to the American Wrestling Association (AWA) in Minneapolis. It was there that he started developing a persona that would become one of wrestling's most imitated. Clothing himself in tie-dye and feathers and flexing his muscles before matches, Graham became an entirely new type of character. He also proved very comfortable with a microphone.

"The main person who influenced me, as far as my promos, was Muhammad Ali," he says. "He was the absolute button that pushed me. He was so incredibly entertaining that I started copying his stuff as far as interviews would go. That over-the-top, 'I'm the greatest' stuff. That really sparked my in-ring personality."

The combination of the look and the talk made Graham into a sensation. It didn't matter that his wrestling skills were in question. Wrestling was turning a corner, and Graham was a herald of a brand-new era of entertainers. Some argue that his success in the early 1970s was a major part of a transformation of the sport that had been ongoing since the birth of television some twenty-five years earlier.

Graham eventually headed south to work in the Dallas-Houston territory—a guy from Arizona could only take the Minnesota cold for so long, after all. While in Texas, he was offered a spot in Vincent J. McMahon's World Wide Wrestling Federation in the Northeast.

From the start, the Superstar was right at home in McMahon's organization, where larger-than-life figures ruled the roost. He was given the equally flamboyant Grand Wizard as a manager. After a successful run, Graham left the territory, which was the norm in those days, but was certain he'd be back to work for McMahon.

In late 1976, Graham went to work for Eddie Graham in his Florida promotion, where he would greatly influence a young fan named Terry Bollea, who would go on to become the most famous wrestler of all time—Hulk Hogan—using a lot of Graham's characteristics and mannerisms.

Meanwhile, back in the Northeast, Vince McMahon Sr. needed a new champion to replace the veteran titleholder Bruno Sammartino, whose career was winding down as his body was starting to suffer the effects of eighteen years of battering. Remembering the colorful Superstar, McMahon thought he might be just the man to pull it off, and contacted old friend Eddie Graham for a meeting. Eddie flew Billy to Vince's Fort Lauderdale home in his private plane, and a deal was worked out to bring the Superstar back as Bruno's top opponent.

Superstar Billy Graham vs. Bruno Sammartino.

Sure enough, Graham walked back into the Federation, and was able to win the Heavyweight Championship from Bruno Sammartino in Baltimore on April 30, 1977.

"They saw something in me, both Vince Sr. and Vince Jr.," says the Superstar. "There were a lot of babyfaces that never got a title shot, because Bruno was a babyface. So it was always heels getting shots. There were guys like Ivan Putski, Gorilla Monsoon, Chief Jay Strongbow, who had never gotten shots. It was an unusual thing, but they decided they could make it work."

For the first time ever, the company's flagbearer was not a hero, but a true ring villain. Previously, the bad guys had mainly wound up being short-term transitional champions, but Graham held the title for ten months, the longest reign for a heel WWE Champion to this day.

"But as it went along," says Graham, "over that ten-month period, I began to do incredible business. And what was happening was the people were beginning to turn me babyface. Fans were popping up all over. My persona was very charismatic, plus very entertaining, so it was hard to hate me."

It all came to a grinding halt on February 20, 1978, in the Garden, when Graham lost the championship to Bob Backlund, a no-nonsense wrestler with amateur credentials.

Graham became very bitter after the loss to Backlund, and entered the darkest period of his career.

"I was very depressed, because I knew I had been in such a perfect situation, and losing that just took the wind right out of me."

He took some years away from the Federation, and completely reinvented himself. Shaving his head and growing a mustache, Graham adopted a karate master persona, casting aside the tie-dyed T-shirts and feathered boas. In 1982, he returned a completely changed man.

"Coming back with that karate gimmick, it was the complete opposite of what I was," he says. "It was really out of depression that I did that gimmick. I didn't have it in me to be the colorful, flamboyant jive-talker anymore, because I felt I had missed the big boat. It was so strange, because people didn't even believe I was the same guy! I got involved with a lot of drugs during that period of time, so I really was in bad shape."

After headlining against Backlund again for a few months, Graham was gone again, this time heading down to Jim Crockett's Carolinas territory. While there, he finally felt comfortable going back to his original Superstar persona. Keeping the shaved head, he broke out the T-shirts and bandannas once again, and added a two-tone beard. The Superstar was back.

By the mid-1980s, Graham began to suffer from a disease called avascular necrosis, in which lack of blood flow to the joints actually causes bones to die. Underestimating the damage his body had suffered, in 1987 Graham resigned with World Wrestling Federation, now in the full bloom of the *Hulkamania* era.

With his physical condition deteriorating, Graham had to curtail his original plans to once again be a Federation headliner. Instead, he was moved into a managerial role, with Don Muraco as his protégé. But even that role, which involved standing at ringside for prolonged periods, proved too much for him. Next, he was made a TV commentator. When the physical exertion of traveling became an impossibility for the ever-worsening Superstar, even the announcing gig had to be dropped. By the end of 1988, Superstar Billy Graham was forced to end his career in sports entertainment at age forty-five.

As if all that wasn't bad enough, Graham was discovered to have hepatitis C while giving blood for a second hip replacement. The possible result of commingling of blood during his years in the ring, the new disease soon began ravaging Graham's liver, and by 2002, he had reached the point of needing a replacement in order to survive.

With literally a few hours left, a suitable donor was finally found in Kate Gilroy, a twenty-six-year-old mother who had been killed in a car accident.

Since then, the Superstar has made an incredible recovery. Although his mobility is still limited from the necrosis, his life is no longer in jeopardy. The depression that had been a side effect of the hepatitis also disappeared.

After years of estrangement from WWE resulting from a falling-out with Vince McMahon in the late 1980s, the Superstar was welcomed back into the WWE family in 2003, when an invitation was extended to attend *SummerSlam* in Phoenix and pay a visit backstage. Since then, he has made several appearances on WWE television, and was finally inducted into the WWE Hall of Fame in 2004 by Triple H. He recently published an autobiography, *Tangled Ropes*.

There's no doubt about it—Superstar Billy Graham has rebuilt his life on every front. In the best physical and mental condition he's been in for years, he's once again a part of the sports entertainment company whose championship he once carried so proudly.

- Bruno once hosted a radio program in New York City, playing records from his own collection.

- Bruno is an avid opera fan, and is particularly fond of Franco Corelli.

- In the 1970s, Bruno was one of a series of sports legends covered in an ongoing TV program hosted by Johnny Bench.

The original WWE World Championship has existed for forty-three years. Bruno Sammartino held it for eleven of those years—more than one-quarter of its history.

On May 17, 1963, Bruno Sammartino began the longest World Championship reign in wrestling history, beating Buddy Rogers by submission in under a minute. And that was only his first of two multiyear reigns. For two decades, he was the literal embodiment of World Wide Wrestling Federation to hundreds of thousands of fans throughout the northeastern United States— then the company's base of operations. Long before Hulk Hogan, he was the invincible force who rallied people behind him each

BRUNO SAMMARTINO

HEIGHT: 5'10"

WEIGHT: 265 lbs.

FROM: Abruzzi, Italy

YEARS IN WWE: 1960–81; 1984–88

CAREER HIGHLIGHTS: 2-time WWWF Heavyweight Champion (1963–71; 1973–77); WWWF U.S. Tag Team Champion (1967, w/Spiros Arion); WWWF International Tag Team Champion (1971, w/ Dominic DeNucci)

FINISHING MANEUVERS: Bearhug; Italian Backbreaker

NICKNAMES: The Living Legend; the Italian Superman

and every time he came out to the ring for one of his countless title defenses.

He was born October 6, 1935, in Pizzoferrato, Italy, a small town in the Appenine Mountains in the Italian province of Abruzzi. One of seven children, Bruno had only two surviving siblings, a brother and sister, by the time World War II broke out in Europe in 1939. His father Alfonso, a blacksmith, had relocated to the United States before Bruno was born in order to find work to support the family. But when the war started, Alfonso was completely cut off from his family. Italy was under the fascist regime of Benito Mussolini, an ally of Adolf Hitler.

The Nazis eventually occupied Pizzoferrato, forcing the Sammartinos to go into hiding to avoid the oppression of SS troops. They spent fourteen months living in a mountain called Valla Rocca. In order to provide food and supplies for her cold and starving children, Bruno's mother Emilia would sneak back into their home some nights and grab whatever she could, often narrowly escaping discovery.

By the time the war was over and Alfonso once again was able to contact his family, Bruno was just skin and bones, having subsisted on a diet often consisting of nothing more than snow and carrion meat. But now at last, the family could be reunited. They took a cargo ship from Naples and, after enduring a tuberculosis quarantine at Ellis Island, arrived in Pittsburgh, Pennsylvania, where Alfonso had settled some years earlier.

A newly arrived immigrant speaking no English, and quite sickly, Bruno had difficulty adjusting to school in America. He was routinely picked on, and as a teenager, determined to rectify the situation by building up his body with weights at the local YMCA. By age eighteen, he weighed 257 pounds, and was already competing in weightlifting contests. Although his father had gotten him a job as a carpenter's assistant, he had already decided that he wanted to use his newfound muscle mass to become a professional wrestler.

In 1955, at the age of nineteen, he met his future wife, Carol, then sixteen. Three days later, he asked her to become his first steady girlfriend, and four years after that, when they had enough money, they were married. They would have their first son, David, in 1960, as well as fraternal twins Danny and Darryl in 1968.

At the time of his marriage, Sammartino was working construction, but just two months after his wedding, he started wrestling.

Some old school friends of his, who were acquainted with Pittsburgh promoter Rudy Miller, got Bruno a tryout, and the Italian muscleman made such an impression that he was started immediately. He debuted in 1959, winning his first match in nineteen seconds. Miller soon brought Sammartino to the attention of Vincent J. McMahon, head promoter for much of the Northeast (what would later become WWWF). McMahon was unsure, but his business partner, the wizened old wrestling mastermind Toots Mondt, convinced him that Bruno could be huge.

He started wrestling on the New York scene in 1960, and was an overnight sensation. Word soon spread of the hot new commodity in wrestling, and Bruno's services were requested elsewhere as well. He was a hit in Toronto, where he spent some months competing for promoter Frank Tunney. A scheduling mishap (Sammartino was accidentally booked in two cities on the same night and unknowingly missed a match) caused him to be suspended by several state athletic commissions, but once the fines were paid by Vince McMahon, Bruno went to work for the New York promoter on a full-time basis.

Sammartino was groomed to be the company's top star, as McMahon hoped his overwhelming popularity would help him break away from the NWA and create his own independent entity. Mere months after WWWF was created in 1963, Sammartino fulfilled his destiny, taking the newly established WWWF Heavyweight title at just twenty-seven years of age.

For more than seven and a half years, he was the unquestioned king. It seemed like he would never lose, and they say that the night he did lose the title in Madison Square Garden to Ivan Koloff, you could hear a pin drop in the arena. The crowd literally could not believe that he had been pinned.

"He was so shocked that night when the crowd went totally

Ivan Koloff vs. Bruno Sammartino.

silent," remembers Dick Kroll, the referee for the match. "The building was sold out, and it was a clean finish in the center of the ring. Koloff jumped off the top rope with a kneedrop, and I counted one, two—and everybody waited for Bruno to get his shoulder up—then I counted three and the place was as silent as a tomb. Bruno went back to the dressing room afterwards and we were talking to each other and he said 'I never saw anything like that.' He couldn't believe the shock of the fans. They were afraid to even present Koloff with the belt, because they thought there might be a riot."

Three years later, he was back in the saddle again as champion, dismantling the top heels of the 1970s, just as he had done to the top heels of the 1960s.

He was a main attraction for twenty years—longer than anyone else in WWE history, even Andre the Giant. Madison Square

Garden was his home field, and he sold it out more times than any other performer in any field of human endeavor. On a nearly monthly basis, hordes of raucous fans packed the Garden to witness their hero's exploits, just as they did in other arenas like the Boston Garden, the Philadelphia Spectrum, and the Capitol Center, and in cities like Pittsburgh, Bridgeport, Baltimore, and Providence.

Those exploits included bodyslamming the 601-pound Haystacks Calhoun, as well as battling fellow fan favorite Pedro Morales before 30,000 people at Shea Stadium. In addition to his Northeast duties, Sammartino was the first WWWF Champion to defend the title overseas, taking on the late Giant Baba in Japan. He also frequently traveled to other territories throughout the United States.

"I traveled all over the world with him," recalls his longtime manager Arnold Skaaland. "He was a great guy. We had a lot of good times together. He loved to eat Italian food. I never ate so much Italian food in my life! We really had a good rapport between us."

He was no great technician, and possessed none of the over-the-top flash of today's top Superstars. Yet few champions before or since possessed his kind of subtle charisma—the ability to get the people behind him, and most importantly, to *believe* in him. Fans invested their emotions in Sammartino, just as they would for any great sports hero.

That fact was put to the test in April 1976, when Bruno suffered a serious injury during a match with Stan Hansen in Madison Square Garden. Slippery with sweat and blood, Sammartino was dropped on his head by Hansen, who was trying to execute a bodyslam. The botched move broke the neck of the champion, who nevertheless continued the match, even after subsequently taking Hansen's brutal lariat clothesline. The match was stopped due to excessive bleeding, and amazingly, Bruno left the ring under his own power. It wasn't until he was found passed out in the locker-room shower that the severity of the injury was discovered. Bruno had come very close to being paralyzed, and spent the next two months in a hospital bed, in traction.

By his own admission, he returned to action way too soon, stepping back in the ring just two months later for a rematch with Hansen in Shea Stadium. Despite not being fully recovered, as well as being unable to train effectively, Sammartino's intensity helped drive him to victory, which occurred when he beat Hansen so badly that the massive Texan fled the ring and was counted out.

"With Bruno, you knew you were really in there with a living legend," says Superstar Billy Graham, the man who ended Sammartino's second title reign in 1977. "The fans' reactions were so tremendous. He was the ethnic, humble Italian, the powerful, beloved, quiet champion. Even though he was soft-spoken, he still conveyed power and confidence."

Sammartino continued for a few years as a top draw after losing the title for the last time in 1977. In 1981 he retired and disappeared from the scene for a number of years. He was brought back as an announcer in 1984 (Bruno had already done some announcing in the latter years of his wrestling career), and even came out of retirement in 1985 to compete part-time for another two years. During this time he often Tag Teamed with his son David, but eventually refused to continue, citing advancing age and accumulated injuries. David's career collapsed shortly thereafter, and Bruno has always claimed that his son blames him for that. The two have not spoken in eighteen years.

Bruno was unhappy with the direction World Wrestling Federation had taken in the era of *Hulkamania,* and much preferred the wrestling of his own day. He also disliked the steroid abuse he believed all too often was taking place among competitors at the time. In 1988 he walked away from the company and, sadly for his many fans, has maintained an ongoing grudge against WWE ever since, refusing to associate in any way with the organization he once represented.

These days, Sammartino and his wife still reside in Pittsburgh. Bruno continues to maintain an excellent physique at age seventy. He is the proud grandfather of nine-year-old Anthony Bruno Sammartino, the child of his son Danny.

If you were a wrestling fan in the Northeast during the 1960s and '70s, the man was a god. The ethnic factor certainly played a big part, as fans of Italian descent (as well as other ethnicities) in places like New York identified strongly with him. His name was one of a pantheon of Italian-American icons that included the likes of Frank Sinatra and Joe DiMaggio. Talk to any fan of that era, and there is no question about it. He may not have had the national stage, but that takes nothing away from his own accomplishments. His achievements as the titleholder have yet to be surpassed. Bruno Sammartino was the greatest World Champion in the history of WWE.

- Brazil is responsible for coining a well-known saying within the industry. When a show failed to sell out, he would remark, "It must be that new all-night gas station they opened in town."

- Brazil and his greatest rival, the Sheik, both entered the sport in the early 1950s, and both left it forty years later in the early 1990s.

- For the last twenty years of his life, Brazil owned a restaurant, Bobo's Grill, in his hometown of Benton Harbor.

A true pioneer of the mat game, Bobo Brazil is often referred to as "the Jackie Robinson of professional wrestling." While he wasn't the first black pro wrestler, he certainly was the first to break out as a major superstar and headliner. During an era when racism was arguably the worst it ever was in the twentieth century, Brazil emerged as one of the hottest names anywhere in pro wrestling. His trailblazing paved the way for such later stars as Ernie Ladd, Tony Atlas, the Junkyard Dog, and Booker T.

He was born Houston Harris in Little Rock, Arkansas, on July 10, 1924. His family moved to East St. Louis, Illinois, before

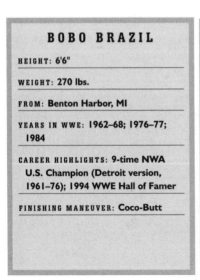

BOBO BRAZIL

HEIGHT: 6'6"

WEIGHT: 270 lbs.

FROM: Benton Harbor, MI

YEARS IN WWE: 1962–68; 1976–77; 1984

CAREER HIGHLIGHTS: 9-time NWA U.S. Champion (Detroit version, 1961–76); 1994 WWE Hall of Famer

FINISHING MANEUVER: Coco-Butt

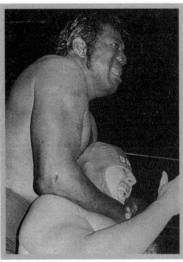

finally settling in Benton Harbor, Michigan, where Harris grew to adulthood.

After being discovered by the great Jumpin' Joe Savoldi, Harris made his debut as a pro wrestler in 1951. When he took the name "Bobo Brazil," it seemed like he was doomed from the start to be just another one of the racial stereotypes that populated wrestling at the time. In addition to the demeaning name, his headbutt finisher was called the Coco-Butt, and TV announcers would sometimes refer to him as a "boy."

But Bobo Brazil rose above all that. His impressive size and natural charisma made him a big hit with fans of all colors, right off the bat. He possessed a class and dignity that few African-American wrestlers were permitted to incorporate into their in-ring personas at the time. Over the course of the 1950s, Brazil established himself as an important name on the wrestling scene.

"He was the first African-American wrestler I knew who was a real top superstar," said Freddie Blassie in his autobiography, *Listen, You Pencil Neck Geeks*. "Even white bigots couldn't help cheering for Bobo. As for black fans, I'm certain they would have skinned me if he'd asked."

In 1956, while competing in San Francisco for promoter Joe Malcewicz, he joined with Latino star Enrique Torres to win that territory's version of the NWA World Tag Team Championship— the original version—from the perennial titleholders, Ben Sharpe & Mike Sharpe. They claimed the title again the following year.

But the territory where Brazil would spend most of his time over the years was Detroit, the one closest to his home. He first won Detroit's version of the NWA U.S. Championship in 1961 from Dick the Bruiser, and would go on to win it another eight times over the next fifteen years. He would also become one of the Detroit area's most beloved sports heroes.

"Bobo was such a classy man," remembers Vince McMahon. "Classy as hell. Understood the business, great psychologist in terms of the business, what worked, what didn't. He loved being the babyface, and getting the sympathy, that sort of stuff. Understanding the psychology of how you put a match together."

His archrival in Detroit was the notorious Sheik, with whom Brazil had countless matches, and they traded the U.S. title back and forth on several occasions. Their war raged for decades, and is still famous today as one of the bloodiest, most enduring feuds the sport has ever seen.

Bobo Brazil first came to work for Vincent J. McMahon's Capitol Wrestling Corporation (the company that would later become WWWF) in 1962. He formed a successful tandem with French Canadian great Edouard Carpentier, facing off against such duos as the Fabulous Kangaroos, and challenging Buddy Rogers & "Handsome" Johnny Barend for the U.S. Tag Team Championship in two consecutive Madison Square Garden main events.

Brazil remained one of the WWWF's top headliners for six years, repeatedly competing at or near the top of the card nearly every single month at the company's main venue, the Garden. He feuded with the likes of Killer Kowalski, Gorilla Monsoon, Freddie Blassie, and Waldo Von Erich, and tag teamed with such popular Superstars as Pedro Morales and Argentina Apollo. He was a frequent Tag Team partner of the young Bruno Sammartino during the time when Bruno was being groomed to be Heavyweight Champion.

Much of Bobo's WWWF time was spent in Tag Teams. He and Dory Dixon were challengers to the U.S. Tag Team Championship held by Skull Murphy & Brute Bernard, and in fact faced the champs in a match that took place right before Sammartino won the WWWF Heavyweight title from Buddy Rogers in 1963. In the fall of 1964, he formed another top team with Haystacks Calhoun, and that duo nearly captured the U.S. Tag Team title from Dr. Jerry Graham & "Crazy" Luke Graham. Another frequent partner was "Sailor" Art Thomas, who joined with Brazil to challenge Gorilla Monsoon & "Cowboy" Bill Watts for the U.S. Tag Team Championship. Brazil also teamed with Johnny Valentine to take on the men who held the gold at the beginning of 1966, the Miller Brothers.

In August 1967 Brazil suffered a rare WWWF loss, and a damaging one at that, falling to Hans Mortier in under a minute. He disappeared from the territory for a few months, and returned briefly the following year. But by that point, as he entered his mid-forties, Brazil's star was waning in WWWF. He had been one of the most consistent main eventers of the 1960s, but that run had come to an end.

Yet even while regularly competing for McMahon, Brazil routinely traveled to other territories, where his services were always in demand. In Los Angeles' World Wrestling Association, for example, he developed a huge fan following and won the WWA Heavyweight title—once one of the most widely recognized in the nation—twice, in 1966 and 1968. His 1968 reign came to an end when the championship was dissolved after the WWA joined the NWA and recognized its World Champion.

Brazil even traveled to Japan after leaving L.A., becoming a major attraction in the Land of the Rising Sun, and winning the International title of the Japanese Wrestling Association, the country's top promotion at the time.

Meanwhile, the feud with the Sheik was waged on and off through it all. The two legends had one of their highest-profile encounters in Los Angeles in 1971, as part of the first wrestling event aired on closed-circuit television. Brazil also passed through the NWA's Central States territory, where he held the Tag Team Championship with Bob Geigel.

At the beginning of 1976, after an eight-year absence, Brazil returned to the WWWF scene, which he had so dominated the previous decade. At the same time, he was also working in Detroit, and when he won his eighth U.S. title there from the Sheik, the level of respect was so high for him in WWWF that he was actually acknowledged there as U.S. Champion, at a time when titleholders from outside territories were never announced as such.

Brazil's 1970s period in WWWF wasn't nearly as eventful as his headlining days in the 1960s, and most of his time was spent defeating mid-carders as opposed to main-eventing. At fifty-plus years of age, it seemed like things were winding down. Yet Brazil had no intention of hanging up the boots anytime soon.

In 1977 he ventured to Jim Crockett's Mid-Atlantic Championship Wrestling, where he defeated Blackjack Mulligan for the most

Bobo Brazil vs. Baron Scicluna.

widely recognized version of the U.S. Championship (the one that later became the WCW U.S. Championship and was revived in WWE). But in August of 1977, in a true "passing the torch" moment, the veteran Brazil lost the title to a newcomer who was on his way up in a big way—"Nature Boy" Ric Flair.

Bobo's main territory in Detroit closed its doors in 1980, but he kept plugging away anyhow for the rest of the new decade. By now one of wrestling's elder statesmen and a bona fide legend, his appearances were highly anticipated events. He teamed with Dusty Rhodes in *his* home territory of Florida to take the Florida Tag Team title from Ivan Koloff & Nikolai Volkoff in 1980. And in May 1984, he made what would turn out to be his final World Wrestling Federation appearance, a one-time-only affair at Madison Square Garden in which he teamed with Rocky Johnson & S. D. Jones to take on the Wild Samoan trio of Afa, Sika, & Samu.

Bobo Brazil continued to compete until well into the 1990s, amazing longtime fans with his longevity and inspiring awe in younger fans who had heard tales of his legend. But as he approached seventy years of age, even the mighty Brazil had to admit the time had come to call an end to an incredible career.

In his last years, Brazil was involved in a lot of charity and community work, just as he had been for much of his active career. On January 14, 1998, he was hospitalized after suffering a series of strokes, and on January 22, he passed away at the age of seventy-four.

Few wrestlers can claim to have changed the sport as much as Bobo Brazil. Breaking down color boundaries far and wide in an arena of sports entertainment that never had much regulation or outside supervision was no mean feat. The degree to which his larger-than-life persona opened up doors in this business for all those athletes of color who came after him cannot be overstated.

- Pedro Morales was Intercontinental Champion for more time combined than anyone else.

- Morales estimates that he is related to 60 percent of the population of his native Culebra; he has sixty-five cousins on his mother's side alone.

Because his nearly three-year reign as WWWF Heavyweight Champion fell between the two historic reigns of Bruno Sammartino, Pedro Morales is often shortchanged by chroniclers of WWE history. Yet to overlook this Latino legend is to do a terrible disservice to modern fans. Morales was arguably the most beloved Latino competitor in American wrestling history, and held the championship proudly for a length of time surpassed only by Sammartino, Bob Backlund, and Hulk Hogan.

Pedro Morales was born October 22, 1942, on the island of Culebra, located seventeen miles east of mainland Puerto Rico. As a child, he developed a keen interest in baseball, and played both centerfield and first base. He almost wound up playing for Puerto Rico's Ponce Lions team, but unfortunately the Lions' recruitment

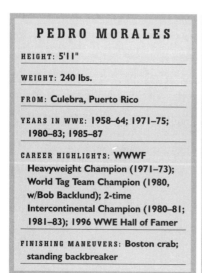

PEDRO MORALES

HEIGHT: 5'11"

WEIGHT: 240 lbs.

FROM: Culebra, Puerto Rico

YEARS IN WWE: 1958–64; 1971–75; 1980–83; 1985–87

CAREER HIGHLIGHTS: **WWWF Heavyweight Champion (1971–73); World Tag Team Champion (1980, w/Bob Backlund); 2-time Intercontinental Champion (1980–81; 1981–83); 1996 WWE Hall of Famer**

FINISHING MANEUVERS: **Boston crab; standing backbreaker**

letter arrived late due to inefficient mail delivery to Culebra. By the time Pedro's mother received it, her son had moved to Brooklyn, New York, to live with his aunt.

To be one of the nearly half-million Puerto Ricans in New York during the 1950s almost invariably meant being fans of Puerto Rico's own Miguel Perez and his popular Italian partner Antonino Rocca, one of wrestling's elite Tag Teams. Morales was no different—as a teenager, he became part of the Rocca & Perez fan club, based in Manhattan.

This affiliation interested him in giving the squared circle a try, and in 1958, at sixteen, Morales had his first match, aired on New York television from one of the first cards presented by Vincent J. McMahon at Sunnyside Gardens in Queens.

For nearly five years, Morales worked hard at establishing himself in McMahon's fledgling Capitol Wrestling Corporation. He mostly competed at some of the smaller venues in the New York area, until January 1963, when he made his Madison Square Garden debut, teaming with his boyhood idol Miguel Perez to take on the Tolos Brothers. Perez's longtime partner Rocca had had a falling-out with promoters McMahon and Toots Mondt, and Morales was used to fill his spot as an ethnic draw—then a very important component of wrestling's appeal, particularly in the Northeast.

In the mid-1960s, Morales formed two successful Tag Teams in the newly established World Wide Wrestling Federation, one with Perez and the other with a Rocca copycat known as Argentina Apollo. Morales & Apollo challenged Skull Murphy & Brute Bernard for the WWWF U.S. Tag Team Championship in 1963, and the Morales-Perez team almost succeeded in taking the gold from Dr. Jerry Graham & "Crazy" Luke Graham the following year.

"Classy" Freddie Blassie, who faced Morales in the Garden in late 1964, was impressed with the young man's abilities, and when Blassie returned to his main stomping grounds in Los Angeles, he persuaded Morales to come with him. In Los Angeles' World Wrestling Association, Morales got a taste of the main event, and became a much bigger star than before.

He beat the masked Destroyer for the WWA Heavyweight Championship in March 1965 and held it for four months before losing it to Luke Graham. In the fall, he regained the prestigious title from Graham and held it for another ten months.

Morales began making the rounds through the nation's territorial wrestling system. He worked for Roy Shire in San Francisco, Ed Francis in Hawaii, and Dory Funk Sr. in Amarillo, Texas.

"Dory Funk Sr. was crazy," remembered Morales, "but he and Gory Guerrero, Eddie's father, were the ones who taught me about being a wrestler. I learned about the show business part of this industry from Pat Patterson, Ray Stevens, and Pepper Gomez when I was in San Francisco."

While in Hawaii, Morales was contacted by McMahon confidant Gorilla Monsoon, who arranged a meeting with the WWWF owner at the Dunes Hotel in Las Vegas. The purpose of the meeting was not only to bring Morales back to WWWF, but to explain that McMahon wanted to make him into a top contender for the Heavyweight Championship.

"I knew what *that* meant," said Morales. "The old man didn't want to make a commitment yet. But he wasn't talking about being a number-one contender. He was talking about the big one."

Morales made his return to Madison Square Garden on January 18, 1971, the very night Bruno Sammartino's seven-year reign as WWWF Champion was ended by "The Russian Bear" Ivan Koloff. Just three weeks later, at the next MSG show, Morales toppled Koloff to become the new Heavyweight Champion.

Ideally, Morales was chosen as the replacement for Bruno Sammartino. Realistically, he never quite escaped the shadow of the Living Legend. Nevertheless, he was an immensely popular champion, particularly in New York, where legions of loyal Puerto Rican fans filled Madison Square Garden every month to root for him, just as Pedro himself had done for Rocca & Perez.

Morales became a hero to New York's Puerto Rican population—which desperately needed one at the time. With one out of every four Puerto Rican families subsisting below the poverty line, and an average family income one-third lower than the average of

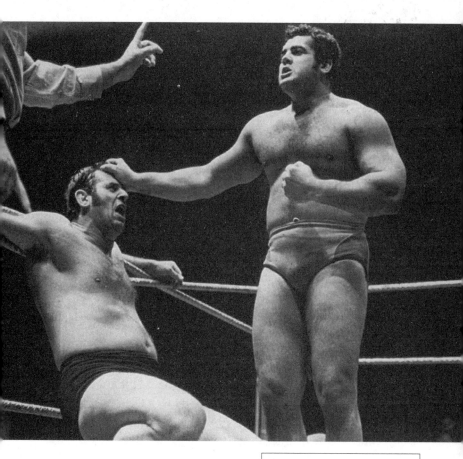

the rest of the city's families, life was not all that bright for the majority of Morales's fan base. And while the champ's monthly victories at MSG could by no means put food on their tables, it certainly accomplished the worthy goal of putting some joy in their hearts nonetheless.

The fiery-tempered Morales would hold the title for thirty-four months, defending it against such ruffians as Baron Mikel Scicluna, Pampero Firpo, George "The Animal" Steele, Ernie Ladd, Ray Stevens, Don Leo Jonathan, and Larry "The Axe" Hennig.

But Morales's most famous match of all would be a title defense against his friend and onetime mentor, Bruno Sammartino. Since bouts between fan favorites were so rare at the time, and these were the top two favorites in the whole company, a special venue was selected: Shea Stadium in Flushing, Queens, the home field of the New York Mets.

"Bruno and I felt the same way [about the match]," Pedro relates. "We were afraid of a revolution between the Italians and the Latinos. But the old man [McMahon] said, 'You're wrong. This is like a fight between brothers. They might try to kill each other in the ring, but they really love each other. And if you do it the right way, the fans will understand that.'"

On September 30, 1972, Morales and Sammartino fought to a seventy-five-minute time limit draw in WWE's first major stadium show. Over 20,000 fans were on hand to witness this mat classic between two of the greatest World Champions of all time.

A little over one year later, on December 3, 1973, Morales lost the title in the Philadelphia Arena to Stan Stasiak in a major upset. Morales had defeated Stasiak before in the past, but on that night, his number was up. He stuck around for another year, but when he found himself slipping down the card, Morales knew it was time to take a break from WWWF.

Morales went into a state of semi-retirement, appearing now and then in various territories. In 1980, he made a dramatic return to the company then known as World Wrestling Federation. His reemergence was met with much fanfare, and it was fitting that on August 9, he teamed with Heavyweight Champion Bob Backlund in Shea Stadium to win the World Tag Team Championship from the Wild Samoans. Although the duo had to give up the title due to bylaws at the time that prevented Backlund from holding two championships at once, Morales had announced to fans that he was back.

Pedro enjoyed his last big run in World Wrestling Federation competing for the newly created Intercontinental Championship. In December 1980 he first won it from Ken Patera, making him the first man to win what was then known as the Federation's "Triple Crown"—the Heavyweight, Tag Team, and Intercontinental titles. He lost the title six months later to the Magnificent Muraco, with whom he waged one of the bloodiest wars of his career. After regaining the Intercontinental gold from Muraco in November 1981, he went on to hold it for nearly fourteen months before losing it back to the Magnificent One.

Shortly after losing his second Intercontinental title, Morales headed down to his native Puerto Rico, where he competed for Carlos Colon's red-hot World Wrestling Council (WWC). In addition to the satisfaction of working in the place of his birth, Pedro also twice held the WWC North American Championship.

In 1985, shortly after the first *WrestleMania*, Morales reentered World Wrestling Federation one last time. This time around, he never reached the same heights he had before. The era of *Hulkamania* had arrived, and Morales seemed to be a relic of a bygone age. He did compete in the WWE-NFL Battle Royal at *WrestleMania 2*, and challenged for the Intercontinental title—against Randy Savage—one last time in his final MSG appearance. After wrestling in the Legends Battle Royal held at the Meadowlands Arena in 1987, Morales called it a career.

Morales stayed on with World Wrestling Federation several more years, working as a Spanish-language TV commentator into the early 1990s. Subsequently, he worked for WCW in the same capacity, and was in fact still under that company's employ when it was purchased by WWE in 2001.

Fully retired, these days Morales enjoys dividing his time between his homes in New Jersey and Puerto Rico. Still a legend among Latino fans in the New York area as well as his native land, Morales takes pride in being the longest-reigning World Champion in WWE history.

- Putski's son Scott was a contender for the World Wrestling Federation Light Heavyweight title in 1998.

- Putski gained his remarkable leg strength by running up and down the stands at a football stadium near his home in Austin, Texas.

- On the mic, Putski would often sing "Melody of Love," a popular song by Polish-American singer Bobby Vinton.

Prior to World Wrestling Federation's mainstream explosion in the mid-1980s, the northeastern territory was populated with an array of ethnic heroes. These Superstars appealed to fans based on where they were born, what race they were, and so forth. In addition to the Italians, Puerto Ricans, Greeks, Irish, and others, there was a Polish immigrant, Ivan Putski, who used his nationality to generate a groundswell of popularity known as "Polish Power."

He was born Joseph Bednarski in the Polish town of Yeuscie Bieskuye, near the Ukrainian border, on January 21, 1941. At the time, Poland had been under the occupation of Nazi Germany for almost a year and a half. In the early 1940s, many Poles were herded into concentration camps, and the Bednarski family was

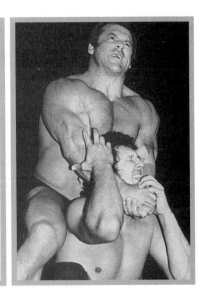

IVAN PUTSKI

HEIGHT: 5'10"

WEIGHT: 242 lbs.

FROM: Krakow, Poland

YEARS IN WWE: 1975–80; 1982–85

CAREER HIGHLIGHTS: World Wrestling Federation Tag Team Champion (1979–80, w/Tito Santana); 1995 WWE Hall of Famer

FINISHING MANEUVER: The Polish Hammer

NICKNAMES: Polish Power; the Polish Piledriver

among them. They were freed in 1945 when the Nazis withdrew from Poland, and five years later, when Joseph was nine years old, they immigrated to the United States, catching one of the last ships bound for Ellis Island.

Joe spent much of his formative years on a farm near Austin, Texas, building his body doing strenuous farm work. He also put that body to use playing football. He played fullback at Southwest Texas State and later considered an offer to play professionally with the NFL's Detroit Lions. In 1968, he was permanently sidelined with an injury that forced him to change his career path. The new path he chose was professional wrestling.

He certainly had the tools for it. When he debuted on the regional Texas scene in 1968, he was a burly strongman with a powerlifter's physique. When he started out in Joe Blanchard's San Antonio territory, he called himself "Jungle" Jim Bednarski, but after heading to the Oklahoma-based promotion run by Leroy McGuirk, he started playing up his Polish origin, taking on the role of a naive and lovable immigrant who spoke only his native language during interviews. He became known in the ring as Ivan Putski. The Mighty Igor, a popular midwestern competitor of the time, was the first to adopt such a persona, but Putski would take it to greater heights.

"There weren't a lot of Poles in Oklahoma," he says. "And I still didn't feel that comfortable with the language. I used to bring my brother Fred with me, just so he could translate if I ran into a hard time. I don't know what it was, but I connected with the people."

He got his first taste of success in Houston working for beloved promoter Paul Boesch. There, he became one of the top box-office attractions, dazzling crowds with his incredible feats of strength. These included tearing up license plates with his hands, crushing oil drums in a bear hug, and holding back a pickup truck with his legs.

In the summer of 1975, he came to World Wide Wrestling Federation, which boasted its fair share of ethnic Superstars, but had never had a Polish one. His popularity carried over without a hitch, and soon the stocky, bearded Putski was in the mix with the cream of WWWF's crop.

"He was one of the top babyfaces in the WWWF doing [that]

Polish gimmick," remembered "Classy" Freddie Blassie in his autobiography. "Chewing on kielbasa and singing Bobby Vinton songs after his victories. He was a muscular guy, and the fans loved him."

Among his frequent opponents was Ivan Koloff, who taunted him with anti-Polish comments. In May 1976 he competed in his first Madison Square Garden main event against Stan Hansen, who the month before had broken the neck of Bruno Sammartino. That summer, at WWWF's second Shea Stadium event, Putski defeated Baron Mikel Scicluna.

When Putski returned to WWWF in the summer of 1978 after a half-year hiatus, his appearance was noticeably changing. He was clean-shaven, and in place of his powerlifter's physique, a ripped bodybuilder's physique was taking shape. He began speaking more English, invoking "Polish Power" on the microphone before his matches.

Summer 1979 found Putski teaming with a young rookie named Tito Santana. On October 22, they beat Jerry & Johnny Valiant in the Garden to win the World Tag Team Championship. They were generally considered the sport's best Tag Team of 1979, and held the title for six months before losing it to the Wild Samoans in Philadelphia.

"I couldn't have picked a better partner," Putski says. "Me and Tito fit together like a hand and glove."

Into the 1980s, Putski continued to be among the most loved Superstars on the roster. He beat Johnny Rodz at the third and final Shea Stadium show in August 1980. After taking his longest sabbatical from WWWF to date—spending over a full year competing in several other territories—Putski returned again in 1982, without missing a beat. He was still a member of the roster at the start of 1984, when Hulk Hogan won the Heavyweight Championship and the Federation began metamorphosing from a regional operation into the dominant force in sports entertainment.

His 1984 feud with Jesse "The Body" Ventura was highlighted by an arm-wrestling contest in which "The Body" gave him a cheap shot. But with the influx of talent from across the country during those early expansion days, Putski had to share the spotlight with

many other popular Superstars, and did not reach quite the same level he had previously achieved.

By the time of the first *WrestleMania,* Putski's star was fading. He did not take part in that historic card, and was more and more relegated to opening matches, his near-perfect record beginning to tarnish. He left the Federation for good at the end of the year and continued making regular appearances throughout the country on the independent circuit for several years before his retirement.

Many of his final appearances were with his son Scott, and in fact in 1997 the "Polish Power" came out of retirement for one last match in World Wrestling Federation, teaming with Scott to take on Jerry "The King" Lawler and his son Brian Christopher on *Raw.*

Over the course of his career, Putski became so beloved that his ethnicity became an afterthought. The charisma and charm of the man himself was enough to make him an all-time great.

- Maivia is featured in the film *You Only Live Twice*, in which he dukes it out with Sean Connery's James Bond.

- Maivia's tattoos, which covered his abdomen and legs, were a symbol of his High Chief status, and were completed in two weeks.

- Maivia purchased the Hawaii wrestling territory from Ed Francis, father of NFL great Russ Francis.

The patriarch of an extended family of Samoan wrestlers, Peter Maivia was one of the most respected competitors of his or any other generation. He came to World Wide Wrestling Federation late in his career, and whether a beloved hero or a vicious rule-breaker, he never failed to attract attention. Although he never lived to see it, he is best known today for the major success of his grandson The Rock, the most electrifying man in sports entertainment.

Maivia was born Leifi Pita Maivia Fanene in 1935 in Samoa. Not long after his birth, the family moved to another island nation, New Zealand, where Fanene was raised. He remained in touch with his native Samoa, where he eventually met his wife, Lia. But it was

HIGH CHIEF PETER MAIVIA

HEIGHT: 6'1"

WEIGHT: 295 lbs.

FROM: Samoa

YEARS IN WWE: 1977–81

CAREER HIGHLIGHTS: 2-time NWA United States Champion (San Francisco version); 2-time NWA World Tag Team Champion (San Francisco version: 1969, w/Ray Stevens; 1974, w/Pat Patterson)

in New Zealand that he made his professional wrestling debut in 1963, soon Anglicizing his ring name to Peter Maivia.

He returned to Samoa often, beginning the process that would eventually see him become a Paramount High Chief, the highest honor a Samoan can achieve. He also spent time training and competing in England during the late 1960s. In Hawai'i, he competed as well as promoted events here and there.

In 1969 Maivia arrived in San Francisco, California, and became one of the territory's hottest attractions. The area had a dense working-class Samoan-American population, and as in many working-class immigrant groups of the era, there was a large concentration of wrestling fans among them. And it was this concentration that turned out in droves to see Maivia wrestle. In those days, he became an inspiration to a new generation of Samoan youngsters who would one day continue the tradition of wrestling's "island boys," always citing Maivia as their main inspiration.

"He was known for being one of the toughest guys around," wrote his grandson The Rock, in his autobiography. "Not in a mean or antagonistic or showy way, but in an honest way. He was just a tough son of a bitch, and if you were smart, you didn't mess with him. . . . But even though my grandfather was the toughest man alive, he was also the sweetest guy you'd ever want to meet. If he was capable of knocking the piss out of you, he was also capable of charming you with a song and a smile."

"I got to meet the chief when I started in Minneapolis," remembers Sgt. Slaughter. "He was the kindest gentleman. Always had a nice thing to say. If Peter Maivia liked you, everyone followed and respected you."

For years, Maivia was a San Francisco staple, winning the area's two top prizes, the NWA U.S. and World Tag Team titles. But he collected more than just titles there; he also collected a son-in-law, Rocky Johnson, a young African-American wrestler. Maivia and Johnson became friendly while both were competing in San Francisco, and Maivia began inviting Rocky back home after the matches. Before long, Johnson had fallen in love with Maivia's daughter Ata, and the two got engaged.

Mr. Fuji vs. Peter Maivia.

"There was just one small problem," wrote The Rock. "Peter Maivia was vehemently opposed to his daughter marrying Rocky Johnson. And so was my grandmother. The reason had nothing to do with his ethnicity, but everything to do with his chosen profession. They disapproved of my dad because he was in the business, and my grandparents knew all about the demons of the business."

But Peter and Lia had no choice but to live with their daughter's decision, and they soon came to warmly accept Johnson into the family. They would become grandparents in May 1972, when Ata gave birth to a son, Dwayne Johnson—the future Rock.

By 1977 Maivia had arrived in World Wide Wrestling Federation, where he was billed as High Chief Peter Maivia—a reflection of his true rank. He drew immediate attention thanks in part to the ceremonial tattoos that covered half his body. At first, Maivia remained a beloved hero as he had always been—until in 1978 he turned violently on Heavyweight Champion Bob

Backlund in a Tag Team encounter, taking on the hated "Classy" Freddie Blassie as his manager. He sealed the deal by also turning at Madison Square Garden against Chief Jay Strongbow, who had been his regular Tag Team partner.

Maivia challenged Backlund in a series of encounters throughout the Northeast, and remained a fixture of the Federation roster for most of the rest of his career. But he still traveled, capturing gold in Los Angeles and nearly winning the NWA World title from Harley Race in New Zealand in 1979.

In 1980, Peter and Lia relocated to Hawai'i and took over the local NWA wrestling territory. Their TV broadcasts were carried throughout the Pacific, as well as the west coast of the United States.

But just as he was making progress with his business, Maivia was diagnosed with inoperable cancer in 1982—after years of suffering from symptoms he hid from those around him.

"The man in that hospital bed looked nothing like my grandfather," wrote The Rock of visiting Maivia during his final days. "The man I knew was a bronzed block of a man, very statuesque and proud and full of life. This man in front of me was someone else. He was frail and withered. He was tired. I walked up and gave him a kiss on the cheek and said, 'Hi, Grandpa. I love you.' But he couldn't respond. I held his hand and looked down at him, waiting for him to flash that big smile of his, the one that could light up the island. But it didn't come."

High Chief Peter Maivia passed away on June 13, 1982, in Honolulu, Hawai'i. His funeral was attended by thousands, and he was laid to rest in Diamond Head, a mountain near the city. His wife, Lia, continued the wrestling promotion until 1988, and remains to this day a respected figure within the business.

In 1996, Maivia's grandson Dwayne debuted in the sport, taking the name Rocky Maivia in honor of his father and grandfather. He would soon shorten it to The Rock, yet go on to honor the High Chief's memory more than ever by becoming one of the most popular mat stars of all time. Although Maivia never got to see it in life, The Rock is certain that he smiles down on him.

- In 1974, Johnson served as a sparring partner for George Foreman during the champ's preparation to fight Muhammad Ali.

- An episode of the hit TV sitcom *That '70s Show* featured Johnson's son, The Rock, playing his father.

- Rocky's brother James also wrestled, under the name Ricky Johnson.

Rocky Johnson may be the father of The Rock, but he was also an accomplished competitor in his own right. An extremely popular black Superstar who traveled the nation pleasing his adoring fans, Johnson has a championship résumé that is just about as extensive as it gets. His chiseled physique helped distinguish him from the start in an era when such a build was far from the norm in wrestling.

He was born Wayde Douglas Bowles in Amherst, Nova Scotia, in 1944, the fourth of five sons born to James Henry Bowles and Lillian Bowles. His family was descended from slaves who had escaped the plantations of the American South by fleeing to

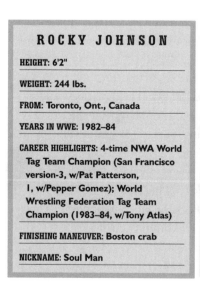

ROCKY JOHNSON

HEIGHT: 6'2"

WEIGHT: 244 lbs.

FROM: Toronto, Ont., Canada

YEARS IN WWE: 1982–84

CAREER HIGHLIGHTS: 4-time NWA World Tag Team Champion (San Francisco version-3, w/Pat Patterson, 1, w/Pepper Gomez); World Wrestling Federation Tag Team Champion (1983–84, w/Tony Atlas)

FINISHING MANEUVER: Boston crab

NICKNAME: Soul Man

Canada in the early nineteenth century. When Wayde was eleven, he and his family moved to Toronto, Ontario, where he would be raised to adulthood.

As a young man, Bowles was interested in both boxing and wrestling, but chose wrestling as something he wanted to seriously pursue. While driving a forklift to earn a living, he would train in his spare time in Hamilton, Ontario, at Jack Wentworth's gym.

In 1964, the already ripped twenty-year-old debuted as a wrestler in the southern Ontario area. He took on the ring name Rocky Johnson, and wound up liking it so much that he soon had his name legally changed. He spent most of the rest of the decade competing in his native Canada, appearing in Toronto, Nova Scotia, and Vancouver, among other places. In Vancouver he won his first championship, the Canadian Tag Team title, teaming with Don Leo Jonathan.

Johnson got his first taste of American competition in Detroit, where he was welcomed with open arms by the city's large African-American fan base. He won Detroit's version of the NWA World Tag Team Championship and moved on to another major American urban center, Los Angeles. There, he captured the area's most prestigious title, the NWA Americas Championship, and in 1970 won the famous L.A. Battle Royal, the most prestigious match of its kind.

The youngster was building momentum and becoming one of the most talked-about newcomers on the scene in some time. He traveled a few miles up to San Francisco, where he remained for several years, building himself into a headliner. He held San Francisco's version of the World Tag Team title on four occasions, three of them with San Francisco mainstay Pat Patterson. The Johnson & Patterson tandem was wildly popular, and the two competed together regularly from 1972 to 1974.

It was while working in San Francisco that Johnson became friends with one of the city's most popular grapplers, High Chief Peter Maivia. The veteran Maivia brought Johnson to his home, where Johnson met the High Chief's daughter, Ata. It was not a storybook romance at first—Rocky thought Ata was snobbish, and Ata didn't appreciate Rocky's tobacco chewing—but they soon fell in love, and were married. On May 2, 1972, their son Dwayne was born.

Johnson's good looks and well-muscled appearance, combined with his dynamic aerial style—he was known as the "King of the Drop Kick"—made him a fan favorite wherever he went. Unlike most of his colleagues, Johnson took his wife and son with him when working in different territories across North America.

The "Soul Man" spent time in Georgia Championship Wrestling, where he held the NWA Georgia Tag Team title with Jerry Brisco. In 1975 he made his way to Championship Wrestling from Florida, where in August he took his first shot at the NWA World Heavyweight title then held by Jerry's brother Jack. When Terry Funk nabbed the gold from Brisco in December, Johnson took another crack at it five days later in Orlando, but failed to capture it.

Johnson headed to the Lone Star State, appearing in both Paul Boesch's Houston Wrestling and Fritz Von Erich's World Class Championship Wrestling out of Dallas. His star shining brighter than ever, he won the Texas Championship and headlined four different times between April and October against World Champion Funk.

By now an experienced veteran himself, Johnson felt the need for a drastic change to freshen up his career. He spent the first two years of the 1980s in a new territory, Mid-Atlantic Championship Wrestling, under a mask, as "Sweet Ebony Diamond." During that time, he won the NWA Mid-Atlantic TV title on two occasions.

In the fall of 1982, Johnson discarded the mask, packed up Ata and ten-year-old Dwayne, and headed north to World Wrestling Federation. At the time, founder Vincent J. McMahon had just sold the promotion to his son Vincent K., a transaction that would change the course of wrestling history.

In a few months, Johnson was among the Federation's top fan favorites, often teaming with the likes of Andre the Giant and Jimmy "Superfly" Snuka. By the spring of 1983, he was the number-one contender for the Magnificent Muraco's Intercontinental Championship. The two met at back-to-back shows

Rocky Johnson vs. Bruiser Brody.

in Madison Square Garden, with neither bout producing a clear winner. The feud culminated in an epic Stretcher match at the Boston Garden.

But the Federation struck gold when it teamed Rocky Johnson with another incredibly popular black athlete, Tony Atlas. Although the two are rumored to have not gotten along personally, in the ring they were dynamite.

Calling themselves the Soul Patrol, Atlas & Johnson opposed the Wild Samoans at a TV taping in Allentown, Pennsylvania, in November 1983, and emerged as the sport's first black World Tag Team Champions. While World Wrestling Federation was transforming as the Bob Backlund era ended and the Hulk Hogan era began, Atlas & Johnson were busy defending their gold against Afa & Sika and other duos like Mr. Fuji & Tiger Chung Lee and David Schultz & Paul Orndorff. They were finally dethroned in April by Adrian Adonis & Dick Murdoch.

The reign of the Soul Patrol was the high point of Johnson's Federation tenure. By late 1984 he was suffering his first major losses in the area to dangerous foes like Schultz and Ken Patera. At the end of the year, mere months before the first *WrestleMania*, Johnson departed.

The Johnson family headed across the Pacific to Hawai'i, where Ata's mother Lia Maivia ran her own highly successful wrestling promotion, left to her by the High Chief, who had passed away in 1982. With his brother Ricky, Rocky Johnson became a regular in Polynesian Wrestling for the next few years. He also was given part ownership in the company, which remained in operation until 1988.

Throwing in the towel on his wrestling career, Johnson moved his family to Florida and shifted his focus to training up-and-coming wrestlers. He had been teaching Dwayne much about the sport since the child was six years old, and by now he was growing into an athletic young man. Nevertheless, Johnson was initially against the idea of his son going into wrestling, and was relieved when it seemed Dwayne was on the path to football stardom as a part of the University of Miami's Hurricanes. He should have known that wrestling was in Dwayne Johnson's blood.

"He had a major influence on me in terms of this industry," The Rock says. "But he came from a different era, a different train of thought. We didn't agree on everything then, as we don't now."

While still training wrestlers and running his own shows in Florida, Johnson watched his son join World Wrestling Federation and become The Rock, perhaps the most well known wrestler of the past decade. The Rock's first WWE name, Rocky Maivia, was obviously a tribute to his famous father and grandfather.

"I knew Dwayne would follow me in the wrestling business," Johnson admits. "Even when he was playing football and everything else, I knew that wrestling was his first love. He's accomplished a lot, and he did it all on his own—blood, sweat, and tears. Everything he has got, nobody has given to him."

Indeed, Johnson has only shared the limelight with his son one time on WWE television, early in The Rock's career. After successfully defending the Intercontinental Championship against the Sultan at *WrestleMania 13*, The Rock was ambushed by the Sultan's comanagers, the Iron Sheik and Bob Backlund. Just when things looked bleak for the Brahma Bull, out came fifty-three-year-old Rocky Johnson to the rescue, as fit as ever. Father and son ran off Team Sultan together, and exulted in a truly rare moment.

In recent years, Rocky Johnson has worked as a trainer, using his Florida facilities as a breeding ground for future Superstars— including current *SmackDown!* competitor Orlando Jordan. It's just the latest chapter of a lifelong dedication to the mat game.

"Once wrestling is in your blood, you never get rid of it," Johnson says. "I never, ever got it out of my system. My father-in-law was that way, and I'm that way—I'm *still* involved in it!"

- Koloff competed in the first-ever Coffin match with **Dusty Rhodes** in Houston, Texas.

- He was one of twenty champions managed by Capt. **Lou Albano**, but the only Heavyweight Champion.

- Koloff is the only man to ever pin **Bruno Sammartino** in Madison Square Garden.

It was a time of cold war, with the United States and the Soviet Union locked in a stalemated struggle for dominance. As the tenets of democracy and dictatorship, capitalism and communism, clashed, and the threat of nuclear annihilation loomed perpetually, fear and animosity reigned supreme. For WWWF fans, that fear and animosity was embodied by one individual: a hulk of a man who represented everything they hated, and who managed to dethrone their greatest hero in one of wrestling's unforgettable moments.

More than anything else, Ivan Koloff—the persona of Ivan

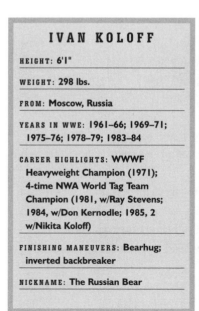

IVAN KOLOFF

HEIGHT: 6'1"

WEIGHT: 298 lbs.

FROM: Moscow, Russia

YEARS IN WWE: 1961–66; 1969–71; 1975–76; 1978–79; 1983–84

CAREER HIGHLIGHTS: **WWWF Heavyweight Champion** (1971); 4-time NWA World Tag Team Champion (1981, w/Ray Stevens; 1984, w/Don Kernodle; 1985, 2 w/Nikita Koloff)

FINISHING MANEUVERS: Bearhug; inverted backbreaker

NICKNAME: The Russian Bear

Koloff—was a symbol. But behind that symbol dwelt a real human being.

He was born Oreal Perras on August 25, 1942, the son of a French-Canadian dairy farmer in rural Quebec.

"There were ten kids in my family," he recalls. "My father was a kind, nice, hardworking man who worked shifts at a coffee plant and on the farm. All we did was work all the time to keep the farm going."

By age eight, he was already hooked on wrestling, following the exploits of Verne Gagne, Pat O'Connor, Hans Schmidt, Fritz Von Erich, and others on TV. Much of what he saw came in handy in roughhousing with his brothers on a regular basis. That, combined with the farm work, helped him bulk up at an impressive rate, and by age fifteen he weighed 200 pounds.

When he turned eighteen, Oreal went to work at a local steel plant, and also started training to become a professional wrestler. When he debuted in 1961, it was under the name Red McNulty. The persona that went with the name was that of a tough Irish thug, with an eye patch and a mean streak a mile wide. He had his first match in the Pittsburgh region of the old WWWF territory. His opponent was none other than the man he'd forever be associated with, Bruno Sammartino.

"I was told in the dressing room by some of the old-timers, 'Kid, if you want to get noticed, you better be aggressive,' " he says. "So when Bruno kneeled down and made the sign of the cross before the match, I started kicking and punching him. He looked up at me like I was crazy. Then he picked me up, slammed me, threw me around, and basically manhandled me. Putting your hands on Bruno when he was making the sign of the cross, that was stepping over the line."

He wrestled as Red McNulty for six years part-time, until he ran into Montreal promoter Jacques Rougeau Sr., who came up with an idea that would make wrestling a full-time career for Perras.

"He asked me if I'd shave my head and come into Montreal as a Russian," he says. "I told him, 'In a New York second.' "

The bearded, burly grappler became known as Ivan Koloff (billed as the nephew of 1920s and '30s wrestler Dan Koloff). He

Ivan Koloff vs. The Iron Sheik.

completely threw himself into the role, taking on a throaty Russian accent and enraging fans by touting the glories of the USSR and denigrating the good ol' U.S. of A. At the time, "Russian" wrestlers were a dime a dozen, but Koloff would soon establish himself as *the* Russian wrestler.

He returned to WWWF in 1969, this time as part of its main circuit. There, he became an instant challenger to Sammartino, by then WWWF Heavyweight Champion. He was initially unsuccessful in his title bid, but that would all change when he made his second go-round a year later.

January 18, 1971, will always be a date that lives in infamy within the hearts of all fans who remember it. Because that was the day that, before the largest Madison Square Garden crowd in eleven years, Ivan Koloff crashed down on Bruno Sammartino with a knee-drop from the top rope and pinned him cleanly in the middle of the ring to end his seven-year reign as Heavyweight Champion. All who were there remember the silence that washed over the stunned crowd that night, and Koloff was not even announced as the new champion for fear of a riot.

The Russian Bear's championship reign would last a mere three weeks, until he was defeated by Pedro Morales at WWWF's next Garden show. Fans horrified that the title had passed to such a despicable character were now pacified, and Koloff departed the scene. He returned to WWWF at various points in the mid-1970s, late '70s, and even the early '80s to challenge Sammartino, and later Bob Backlund, for the title, but would never duplicate the feat.

In the mid-1980s, Ivan enjoyed a lengthy run in the NWA's Carolinas territory. At the time, he formed a successful Tag Team with a man who was billed as his nephew and who became a more muscular 1980s version of the Russian Bear: Nikita Koloff. But in 1989, once the territory was purchased by Ted Turner and turned into WCW, Ivan elected to leave instead of relocating from his North Carolina home to WCW's Atlanta home base.

Koloff continued to wrestle on the independent circuit before retiring from full-time competition in 1994. Although he still steps in the ring every now and then at age sixty-two, his main passion for the past eight years has been his born-again Christianity, which he feels helped save him from the pitfalls that life on the road had created for him. He and his wife still live in North Carolina, but Koloff frequently travels as part of his Christian ministry, preaching and raising money for charity.

A most unusual fate for the Soviet menace who once angered and terrified wrestling fans far and wide.

- Fuji was known for his penchant for relentlessly ribbing his fellow wrestlers.

- Before joining with Paul Bearer in 1991, Undertaker was briefly managed by Fuji.

- In 1977, Fuji was permanently banned from the state of California for walking out on San Francisco promoter Roy Shire and abandoning his NWA U.S. title.

Along with their German, Russian, and Arab counterparts, Japanese villains were a regular part of the wrestling scene for decades. It seemed like wrestling fans were a lot slower to forget the 1941 bombing of Pearl Harbor than other Americans. Many Japanese competitors took advantage of that hatred, and played it up by creating stereotypically devious, conniving ring personas. If they weren't actually Japanese, being Asian, or at least of Japanese descent, was usually enough for them to pull it off. Such was the case for Mr. Fuji, indisputably the most durable and memorable Japanese menace in WWE history.

He was born Harry Fujiwara on May 4, 1945, in Hawaii. By the tender age of fourteen, he had already begun wrestling profes-

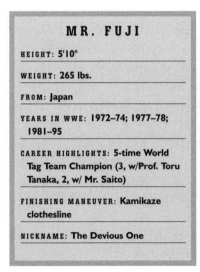

MR. FUJI

HEIGHT: 5'10"

WEIGHT: 265 lbs.

FROM: Japan

YEARS IN WWE: 1972–74; 1977–78; 1981–95

CAREER HIGHLIGHTS: 5-time World Tag Team Champion (3, w/Prof. Toru Tanaka, 2, w/ Mr. Saito)

FINISHING MANEUVER: Kamikaze clothesline

NICKNAME: The Devious One

sionally in his home state for promoter Al Karasick. He slowly worked his way up the card, until in 1965 at the age of nineteen, he captured his first title, the Hawai'ian Tag Team Championship, with King Curtis Iaukea.

He came to the mainland United States in 1966, but it wasn't as Harry Fujiwara that he debuted. Although born in America, he decided to play up his family heritage and billed himself as hailing from Japan. He took on the villainous characteristics American fans expected of Japanese competitors, and became known as Mr. Fuji, a tip of the hat to Mr. Moto, the original and most famous Japanese heel at the time (also Hawai'ian by birth).

Fuji spent much of the late 1960s and early '70s in the Pacific Northwest, but in 1972 traveled to the other side of the country to work in World Wide Wrestling Federation. There he formed a Tag Team with yet another Japanese-Hawai'ian, Professor Toru Tanaka. This partnership would take up most of the remainder of his wrestling career.

"The two certainly had no great admiration for one another," wrote their later manager "Classy" Freddie Blassie in his autobiography. "Fuji was certainly a good performer, but you couldn't control him. So, in addition to worrying about their opponents, Tanaka had the responsibility of making sure that Fuji didn't get out of hand."

Regardless of the fact that Tanaka may have had to keep his eye on Fuji to ensure that he didn't mess things up for both of them, the team was magic from the start, with Tanaka providing the raw muscle and Fuji a mastery of ring psychology. In June 1972, the Grand Wizard led them to the WWWF World Tag Team title with a win over Chief Jay Strongbow & Sonny King. While one half of the champions, Fuji was granted a shot at WWWF Heavyweight Champion Pedro Morales, and the Fuji/Tanaka tandem even took on Morales & Bruno Sammartino in the main event at Madison Square Garden. Finally, in May 1973, Tony Garea & Haystacks Calhoun would end Fuji & Tanaka's reign at one month short of a year.

"Mr. Fuji taught me quite a lot when I was young," remembers Garea. "I would say he probably taught me as much as anybody.

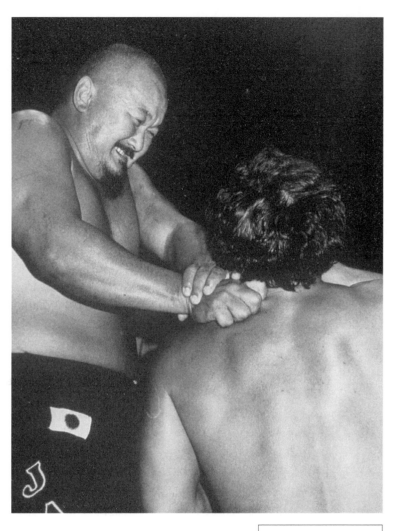

Mr. Fuji vs. Jose Gonzales.

We had different personas, but there was a lot he was able to teach me how to do properly, to fine-tune. He always had so much heat, even if the memories of the war were starting to wear off by then. I think even in the sixties people still thought, if you're Japanese you're an evil person. Once it reached into the seventies, it started to slacken off. But Fuji was a businessman, and was playing a role. He was a family man, really."

In September 1973, Fuji & Tanaka upended Garea & Calhoun, becoming the first duo to regain the title. They held it another two months before losing it to Garea and his new Tag Team partner, Dean Ho. The Japanese terrors departed WWWF shortly thereafter.

Fuji & Tanaka returned to WWWF in 1977 under Blassie's management. In September, they reclaimed the vacant World Tag Team title in a tournament final over Tony Garea & Larry Zbysko. As three-time champions, they set a record that stood for over twenty years before being broken in 1999 by the New Age Outlaws.

Fuji & Tanaka finally split for good in 1979. On his own again, Mr. Fuji spent time competing in New Zealand, Puerto Rico, the Mid-Atlantic, and Canada before returning to World Wrestling Federation in 1981. This time, he had a new Tag Team partner, Mr. Saito (a native-born Japanese). With Capt. Lou Albano as their manager, Fuji & Saito captured two World Tag Team titles, at the expense of Tony Garea & Rick Martel and the Strongbows.

In 1985, Mr. Fuji made the switch from wrestler to manager. Donning a bowler hat and tuxedo, he became even more hated than before, earning the nickname "The Devious One." His first charge was George "The Animal" Steele, and he also managed men like the Magnificent Muraco, Kamala, the Orient Express, Killer Khan, and Sika. He led Demolition to the longest World Tag Team title reign in WWE history.

Perhaps his greatest find of all was the mammoth Yokozuna, whom Fuji brought to the Federation in 1992. Switching from tuxedo to traditional Japanese garb, Fuji (along with American spokesperson Jim Cornette) took Yoko all the way to the Heavyweight Championship with victories over Bret Hart at *WrestleMania IX* and Hulk Hogan at the *King of the Ring 1993*. He later managed Yokozuna & Owen Hart to the same World Tag Team title he had held on five occasions.

After Yoko & Owen Hart lost the title in 1995, Mr. Fuji retired from the business completely, citing health problems that were making travel difficult. He currently resides in Lenoir City, Tennessee, close to his family and friends, and runs a wrestling school in nearby Knoxville—a far cry from Tokyo.

- Nikolai got his ring name from the original Nikolai Volkoff, a Russian wrestler of the 1950s.

- Volkoff was the first competitor managed by "Classy" Freddie Blassie.

- On 1985's *The Wrestling Album*, Volkoff recorded his own version of the Gary "U.S." Bonds song "Cara Mia."

During the height of the Cold War, wrestling captured the spirit of the times by creating a veritable army of Soviet villains, who raised the ire of crowds and propelled them to cheer the opposing heroes to victory. During this era, there was no more durable Red menace than Nikolai Volkoff, the burly matman known for belting out the national anthem of the USSR before his matches. A regular from the 1960s through the '90s, he is one of only a handful of individuals to compete in WWE in four different decades.

"His character was something that people always latched on to and felt strongly about," explains Sgt. Slaughter of his old rival Volkoff's longevity. "He always entertained the people."

Volkoff was born Josip Peruzovic on October 14, 1947, in the eastern European nation of Yugoslavia, the son of a Russian mother

NIKOLAI VOLKOFF

HEIGHT: 6'7"

WEIGHT: 315 lbs.

FROM: Moscow, Russia

YEARS IN WWE: 1968–74; 1976–77; 1979; 1984–88; 1990–92; 1994–95

CAREER HIGHLIGHTS: International Tag Team Champion (w/Geto Mongol, 1970–71); World Tag Team Champion (w/Iron Sheik, 1985); 2005 WWE Hall of Famer

FINISHING MANEUVER: Russian Bearhug

and Croatian-Italian father. As a young man, he achieved local fame as an amateur wrestler and bodybuilder. Anxious to get away from the Communist regime of their country of residence, the Peruzovic family escaped Yugoslavia in the 1960s and made the United States their new home.

At age twenty, the barrel-chested young man decided to help support his family by becoming a professional wrestler. In 1968, he began in the Pittsburgh wrestling promotion, then a satellite promotion of World Wide Wrestling Federation. Due presumably to his size and similar athletic background, his first match was a nontitle encounter with WWWF Heavyweight Champion Bruno Sammartino.

After working as a relative unknown for two years, he received the call from Vince J. McMahon to join the main WWWF roster. He and fellow undercarder Tony Newberry were given the characters of Bepo & Geto Mongol, respectively. With outlandish hairstyles, long mustaches, and animal-skin attire, the Mongols very closely resembled the barbarian tribesmen they were named for. On June 15, 1970, they won the WWWF International Tag Team title from Victor Rivera & Tony Marino in their Madison Square Garden debut. In the fall of that year, Peruzovic, aka Bepo, faced Sammartino in back-to-back cards at the Garden. The Mongols would hold their belts for a year and three days before finally being dethroned by Sammartino & Dominic DeNucci.

In July, the Mongols regained the International tag title, but then WWWF created its current World Tag Team title, with the first champs being Tarzan Tyler & "Crazy" Luke Graham. Tyler & Graham beat the Mongols in a unification match in November, and Bepo & Geto were promptly sent back to Pittsburgh.

At the end of 1973, Peruzovic was brought back to New York, but with an entirely new gimmick and name.

"They made me into a Soviet bad guy," he explained in Fred Blassie's autobiography. "I didn't like the gimmick. I told [my manager] Blassie, 'I don't want to be a bad guy. Yugoslavia's a communist country, and I couldn't wait to escape. I hate communism.'

Bruno Sammartino vs. Nikolai Volkoff.

Blassie said, 'Well, if you hate those bastards, what's the best way to insult them? Show people how bad they are.'"

Renamed Nikolai Volkoff, he immediately entered into a heated feud with still-reigning champ Bruno, engaging in a series of matches in the spring of 1974, including a fifty-three-minute draw at MSG.

Volkoff's knowledge of the Russian language from his mother helped him play the part to a T. Yet beneath the hated Russkie persona was a warm-hearted family man that only his colleagues knew.

"One thing I respected about Nikolai was his devotion to his family," said Blassie. "He had two daughters, and he looked at the wrestling business as a way to pay for their college educations. Instead of eating in a restaurant, he'd buy a bag of groceries and cook in a hot plate in his room. If his pants ripped, he pulled out a needle and thread and darned it. He wouldn't spend a penny to see Jesus Christ jump down Main Street on a pogo stick."

Volkoff's act became popular, and he took it to other territories, though he always made it a point to return to WWWF, where he had first made his name. In 1976 he challenged Sammartino again, and donned a mask as the third member of the Executioners Tag Team. He came back again in 1979 to tangle with then ex-champion Sammartino a third and final time.

In the early 1980s, Volkoff spent most of his time away from the Northeast, sticking to the southern territories. While working in Bill Watt's Mid-South Championship Wrestling, he added a new wrinkle to his routine, whipping crowds into furious frenzies by singing the Soviet National Anthem before his matches. When he finally returned to the nationally expanding World Wrestling Federation in 1984, he brought this new element with him.

As if he wasn't despised enough, Volkoff joined forces with the Iranian Iron Sheik, once again under Blassie's management. At the first *WrestleMania* in March 1985, they beat Mike Rotundo & Barry Windham to take the World Tag Team title, and kept it away from the American duo until the summer. Volkoff's anti-American antics made him one of the most high-profile characters of the *Hulkamania* era, and he even became a top challenger to Hogan.

The Volkoff & Sheik teaming came to an end in 1987 when the Sheik was fired. Nikolai was teamed with another Soviet baddie, Boris Zhukov, as the Bolsheviks. Under the tutelage of the "Doctor of Style" Slick, they teamed for three years, but never experienced much success, most notably losing to the Hart Foundation in nineteen seconds at *WrestleMania VI*.

With the USSR crumbling at the start of the 1990s, Volkoff transformed himself from a hated Communist to a sympathetic ambassador of goodwill. He teamed with former enemy "Hacksaw"

Jim Duggan and feuded with the turncoat Sgt. Slaughter. After taking part in the *Royal Rumble 1992*, he faded out of Federation competition.

After some investments turned sour in the early 1990s, the forty-seven-year-old Volkoff made an unexpected comeback in 1994 as a member of Ted DiBiase's Million Dollar Corporation. Not one of Volkoff's career highlights, this stint saw him being constantly humiliated by DiBiase, who made him his manservant. In mid-1995, Volkoff quit the Corporation and was not seen in WWE again until his 2005 induction to the Hall of Fame. These days, he works as a code-enforcement inspector for Baltimore County, Maryland, and also has been known to occasionally put the boots back on for small independent shows.

Even though it didn't end on a high note, Nikolai Volkoff's WWE career was one of the most enduring ever, spanning the eras of Bruno Sammartino, Hulk Hogan, and Bret Hart. With Soviet heavies a relic of sports entertainment's past, Volkoff represents an earlier time, when nationality and ethnicity played a big role in the landscape of the sport.

- A Palestinian rapper has adopted the stage name "The Iron Sheik."

- Those in the same pro wrestling training camp with the Sheik included Ric Flair, Ken Patera, Jumpin' Jim Brunzell, and Olympian Chris Taylor.

- After winning the Heavyweight title in 1983, the Iron Sheik was featured on the cover of an Iranian newspaper in Los Angeles.

Contrary to popular belief, controversy is not a recent trend in sports entertainment—it's been an integral part of it for many years. In an earlier generation, the Iron Sheik was one of the most controversial figures the sport has ever known. He was also one of the most entertaining. Taking advantage of American-Iranian hostilities, he crafted an unforgettable ring persona. Although the majority of his WWE years occurred during the later *Hulkamania* era, the fact that he was the man to end Bob Backlund's six-year reign as Heavyweight Champion is enough to warrant his inclusion here.

He was born Hussein Khosrow Vaziri in Tehran, Iran, on March 15, 1939. Wrestling was his main interest from childhood, and he was a champion at the high school and college level. He

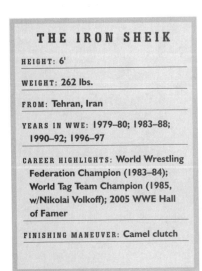

THE IRON SHEIK

HEIGHT: 6'

WEIGHT: 262 lbs.

FROM: Tehran, Iran

YEARS IN WWE: 1979–80; 1983–88; 1990–92; 1996–97

CAREER HIGHLIGHTS: World Wrestling Federation Champion (1983–84); World Tag Team Champion (1985, w/Nikolai Volkoff); 2005 WWE Hall of Famer

FINISHING MANEUVER: Camel clutch

entered the Iranian Army, becoming a national wrestling champion there, as well. His combat skills were so renowned that during the 1960s Vaziri served as a bodyguard for Mohammed Reza Pahlavi, the shah of Iran.

He was a backup member of the Iranian wrestling team at the 1968 Summer Olympics in Mexico City, as well as a two-time Asian freestyle champion. After defecting to the United States in 1970, he won multiple Amateur Athletic Union (AAU) championships. In 1972, he was assistant coach for the U.S. Olympic wrestling team. These impressive credentials, along with Vaziri's reputation for intense physical training, caught the attention of American Wrestling Association (AWA) promoter Verne Gagne, who preferred legitimate grapplers for his professional league.

In 1973, Gagne trained Vaziri for the ring, and he debuted in the AWA. At first, he used his real name and had nothing in the way of a gimmick. But when the need arose to spice up his image, he decided to play up his Iranian heritage to the hilt. He shaved his head, grew a handlebar mustache, and began wearing traditional Muslim garments to the ring, calling himself the Great Hussein Arab.

"I was a bad man in the ring," he remembers. "But all the intelligent wrestling fans respected me because they knew I was a real wrestler."

The persona grabbed instant attention from fans who disliked the way he would routinely badmouth the U.S.A. in his thick Farsi accent. And although fully transformed into a colorful pro wrestler, he even took a time-out to coach the U.S. Olympic team again in 1976.

In the spring of 1979, the Great Hussein Arab arrived in World Wrestling Federation. In his first night at Madison Square Garden, he won a twenty-man battle royal to earn the right to challenge Heavyweight Champion Bob Backlund in the main event that night. He spent most of the next year taking on such opponents as Bruno Sammartino and Chief Jay Strongbow. In early 1980, he departed to compete in other territories.

In the fall of 1983, he was brought back to World Wrestling

Federation, this time as the Iron Sheik. By then, the United States had already been involved in a hostage crisis perpetrated by Iran, and American sensitivities ran high regarding the Middle Eastern nation. The Iron Sheik took full advantage, waving a flag bearing the visage of Iranian leader Ayatollah Khomeini and shouting "Iran Number One!" before his matches.

"It was a good gimmick," says the Iron Sheik. "The ayatollah had a lot of heat in those days. I speak Farsi and am a genuine Iranian. It was a natural."

On December 26, 1983, the Iron Sheik challenged Backlund for the title at MSG. Backlund had previously injured his neck trying to lift the Iron Sheik's Iranian exercise clubs. When he found himself trapped in the Iron Sheik's dreaded camel clutch submission hold, he still refused to submit, and it took his manager Arnold Skaaland throwing in the towel to end the match. The unthinkable had happened: The hated Iron Sheik had ended the Backlund era and was champion of the world.

As it turned out, Sheik was merely a transitional champion, dropping the title one month later at the Garden to the recently returned Hulk Hogan, signaling the end of the Federation's territorial days, and the beginning of its transformation into the modern-day international sports entertainment entity it is today. But things might have turned out differently if the Iron Sheik hadn't made a critical decision.

"Verne Gagne offered me $100,000 to break Hulk Hogan's leg, and take the belt to the AWA," he recalls. "I said, 'I'll let you know in twenty-four hours.' But Vince McMahon Sr. was so nice to me, God bless him. I could not hurt the hand that fed me. I did not double-cross the company."

After losing the title, the Iron Sheik began a memorable war with the superpatriotic Sgt. Slaughter, headlining arenas throughout the summer of 1984 with a series of red-hot matches. The Sheik/Slaughter feud was so successful that it was often the main event at cards that didn't feature Hulk Hogan. By the end of the year, he had joined forces with the Russian Nikolai Volkoff to form one of wrestling's most notorious tandems.

The Sheik vs. Tito Santana.

Under the management of "Ayatollah" Freddie Blassie, Sheik & Volkoff took the World Tag Team title from Mike Rotundo & Barry Windham at the first *WrestleMania* in 1985, and held it for nearly three months. Sheik continued teaming regularly with Volkoff until mid-1987, when he was fired after being arrested for marijuana possession in a story that made national headlines at the time. He briefly returned in 1988, most notably competing in the battle royal at *WrestleMania IV,* but didn't stay long.

After spending a little time in WCW, the Iron Sheik turned up in the Federation again in late 1990. This time he was known as Colonel Mustafa. Much was ironic about this stint: for starters, Mustafa was an ally of the turncoat Sgt. Slaughter, his former enemy, and secondly, he was portrayed as an Iraqi—one of the real-life enemies of Iran.

When Slaughter reembraced his country in 1992, it left Colonel Mustafa with nothing to do, so he unceremoniously departed the Federation. Four years later, when the mysterious masked Sultan (later known as Rikishi) needed a manager, the Iron Sheik united with former foe Bob Backlund and returned to the Federation to fill the role. When the Sultan disappeared from the scene in 1997, so did the Iron Sheik.

For most of the past decade, he's continued to wrestle on a full-time basis on the independent circuit. In 2001, Vince McMahon called him back one last time to take part in the Gimmick Battle Royal at *WrestleMania X-Seven* in the Houston Astrodome. At the age of sixty-two, he emerged victorious over all the other old-timers, but when the match was over, cocombatant Sgt. Slaughter saw fit to slap the Cobra Clutch on him anyway for old time's sake.

Recent years have seen the Sheik in the news on a couple of occasions. In 2002, he was detained at a Rochester airport under suspicion of being a terrorist. And on May 5, 2003, his twenty-seven-year-old daughter, Marissa, was allegedly strangled to death by her live-in boyfriend.

The story of the Iron Sheik is a testament to sports entertainment's great tradition of creating controversy and courting strong emotions from its fans. His was one of the most famous characters to ever come through WWE.

TOSSING IN TANDEM:
THE TAG TEAM GREATS

- As payment for his first match, Eddie Graham received a twenty-five-pound turkey.

- Dr. Jerry Graham was the favorite wrestler of WWE chairman Vince McMahon when he was a kid.

- In November 1957, Jerry Graham provoked the worst riot in Madison Square Garden history.

WWE has had its share of flamboyant Tag Teams, but the ones to first break that ground were the original Graham Brothers, Dr. Jerry Graham & Eddie Graham. In the late 1950s, they were the two most hated men on the roster, and as drawing stars were exceeded only by Antonino Rocca. And although after their breakup it seemed their careers had spun off in two completely different directions, in the end it was the same personal demons that destroyed them both.

The first of what would become an extended Graham "family" was Jerry Graham. Born Jerry M. Matthews on December 16, 1921,

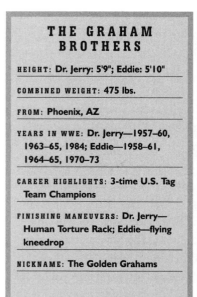

THE GRAHAM BROTHERS

HEIGHT: Dr. Jerry: 5'9"; Eddie: 5'10"

COMBINED WEIGHT: 475 lbs.

FROM: Phoenix, AZ

YEARS IN WWE: Dr. Jerry—1957–60, 1963–65, 1984; Eddie—1958–61, 1964–65, 1970–73

CAREER HIGHLIGHTS: 3-time U.S. Tag Team Champions

FINISHING MANEUVERS: Dr. Jerry— Human Torture Rack; Eddie—flying kneedrop

NICKNAME: The Golden Grahams

in Phoenix, Arizona, he went on to become one of the most outrageous characters to ever make a living at the wrestling game.

He debuted in 1947, but didn't start making waves until the 1950s. During a period when outlandish gimmicks and larger-than-life personas were taking over thanks to the advent of television, Jerry became one of those larger-than-life individuals, dying his hair platinum blond, dressing in sequined outfits, and calling himself Dr. Jerry Graham.

A short, stocky spitfire who reveled in the hatred of the masses, Graham was in a class by himself. He lived fast, drove fancy cars, and was infamous for his love of booze and women, in equal amounts.

"Jerry was a crazy character, to put it mildly," remembers former referee and wrestler Dick Kroll. "When I was still wrestling, he once drove me to Asbury Park in his red Cadillac convertible. Graham got stopped by the cops for driving on the sidewalk. He was trying to grab the ass of one of the women walking on the street! Once the cop realized it was Jerry Graham, he gave us a stern warning and let us go on our way. But he was a wild guy."

In 1957, Graham was brought to the Northeast by promoter Vincent J. McMahon, then in the midst of becoming the dominant force in the region. Graham quickly became a top attraction, and adjusted quite nicely to the flashy big-city lifestyle.

"Riding around in 1959 with Dr. Jerry Graham was something else," says WWE chairman Vince McMahon, then just a teenager. "He'd come to D.C. with that bloodred Cadillac convertible, with great big fins on it. He'd say, 'You wanna go for a ride, kid?' I'd say, 'Sure!' He'd ride around with the top down, through the worst section of town. He never stopped at red lights, he'd just blow his horn. Tip his ashes off his cigar and yell some obscenity to anyone that would listen. Watching him light cigars with hundred-dollar bills in 1959 was like, 'Holy shit!' Who wouldn't wanna live like that? He was living a lie, but who knew it? The poor bastard, he would come to Madison Square Garden, where more times than not, he'd headline. By the same time the next night, he'd be broke. He'd blow his entire Garden payoff in one night."

In the summer of 1958, a partner would be found for the good doctor, and wrestling history would be made.

Edward T. Gossett was born in 1929 in Chattanooga, Tennessee. He too had made his in-ring debut in 1947. After eleven years, he caught his first break in 1958, competing as Rip Rogers for Houston promoter Morris Sigel. Later that year, he was contacted by Vince J. McMahon to take part in the Tag Team that would immortalize him.

McMahon brought Gossett to New York and renamed him Eddie Graham. His hair dyed platinum to match his partner, he was billed as Dr. Jerry's brother. With the sheer animosity the fans had for Jerry and his obnoxious manager Bobby Davis, there was certainly enough for him to share with his "brother." The new team was unique at the time, although the basic template would give rise to countless imitators over the next half century.

"They had the most heat," says Kroll. "They were the top heel team. One night the Graham Brothers wrestled Miguel Perez & Hercules Cortez, and they got such heat that the fans tried to kill them. They were barricaded inside the locker room with the fans trying to get in. I had to ride home with Jerry Graham that night, so we made a run for the alley where the car was parked and just jumped in and took off."

In September 1958, they bested the popular duo of Mark Lewin & Don Curtis for their first U.S. Tag Team title. WWE's first championship, the U.S. Tag Team title gave the Grahams instant credibility. Although they lost it three months later back to Lewin & Curtis, they regained it in May 1959 in Bridgeport, Connecticut.

Through all this, Dr. Jerry & Eddie waged the defining war of their Tag Team career, against Antonino Rocca & Miguel Perez. For two years, their matches were the hottest ticket in New York. They met an amazing seven times in the main event at Madison Square Garden during that time.

They lost the gold in April 1960 to the Bastien Brothers, Red & Lou, but would enjoy one more brief reign later that month.

After that point, the two drifted apart. Jerry departed the territory at the end of the year, and Eddie did the same in 1961. In

1963, Jerry returned on his own. He became a top contender for Bruno Sammartino's Heavyweight title, and opposed the champ in three hotly contested MSG matchups. A new "brother" was introduced in 1964, "Crazy" Luke Graham, who periodically teamed with Jerry, and even held the U.S. Tag Team title with him. At the end of the year, Eddie made a brief return to the region, reuniting the original Grahams for another four months before they went their separate ways for good.

Things changed quickly for both of them after that. By the start of the 1970s, they couldn't have gone in more opposite directions. Eddie settled in Tampa, Florida, where he took over the regional wrestling operation from Clarence "Cowboy" Luttral and created one of the most highly regarded territories of all time, Championship Wrestling from Florida. Jerry, meanwhile, spiraled out of control. Years of spending money he didn't have, of overeating and overdrinking, were catching up to him. Bankrupt and morbidly obese, he looked for any way to regain his momentum, including introducing a fourth and final "brother" to the game, Superstar Billy Graham.

As one of the NWA's top promoters—and NWA president for a time—Eddie Graham produced some of the biggest stars the sport has ever seen, including Dusty Rhodes, Jack & Jerry Brisco, and Barry Windham. He had a strong working relationship with Vincent J. McMahon and WWWF, which developed into something of a talent exchange program. He also became a community leader, participating in countless charities and funding public schools.

But all was not as it seemed. For although he didn't show it as his former Tag Team partner did, Eddie Graham, too, struggled with a serious drinking problem. He also suffered from depression. On January 20, 1985, Edward Gossett shocked the Tampa community and the wrestling world by shooting himself to death in his Florida home at age 55.

Jerry attempted a World Wrestling Federation comeback in 1984. Vincent K. McMahon wasn't a kid anymore; he'd taken over from his father and wanted his childhood hero to be a part of the national company he was building. But by that point Jerry had nearly ruined himself, and didn't last more than a few weeks. He spent most of the next dozen years eking out what living he could on the independent circuit as a manager, before passing away of a heart attack on January 24, 1997, at age seventy-five.

Although it ended in tragedy for both parties, the Graham Brothers' legacy is something that grew to be bigger than either one of them. The Valiants, the Fabulous Freebirds, the Rougeau Brothers, Edge & Christian, Billy & Chuck, and untold others would never have existed without them. They made a mark on the sport that will continue to be felt for generations to come.

- Johnny Valiant has appeared on such TV shows as *The Sopranos* and *Law & Order: Criminal Intent*.

- In his later years as "The Boogie Woogie Man," Jimmy Valiant used "The Boy from New York City" as his entrance music.

- One of wrestling's most notorious cases of bad blood exists between the Valiants and their first manager, Bobby "The Brain" Heenan.

Brother Tag Teams abound throughout wrestling history, but no other brother team in WWE history made as much of an impact as the Valiant Brothers, Johnny & Jimmy. It's ironic, then, that they weren't actually blood brothers at all, but brothers by design, who used a good-as-gold gimmick to create a truly memorable legacy. It's all par for the course in the unpredictable world of sports entertainment, where nothing is ever as it seems.

The first of the two to appear in the WWWF was Johnny. Born Thomas Sullivan in Pittsburgh, Pennsylvania, in 1946, he became acquainted with Vincent K. McMahon, current WWE chairman and the son of then–WWWF owner Vincent J. McMahon, when

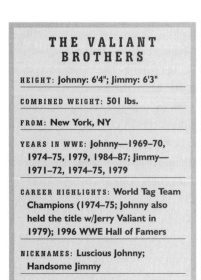

THE VALIANT BROTHERS

HEIGHT: Johnny: 6'4"; Jimmy: 6'3"

COMBINED WEIGHT: 501 lbs.

FROM: New York, NY

YEARS IN WWE: Johnny—1969–70, 1974–75, 1979, 1984–87; Jimmy— 1971–72, 1974–75, 1979

CAREER HIGHLIGHTS: World Tag Team Champions (1974–75; Johnny also held the title w/Jerry Valiant in 1979); 1996 WWE Hall of Famers

NICKNAMES: Luscious Johnny; Handsome Jimmy

the two were students together at the Fishburne Military Academy in Waynesboro, Virginia.

"We played basketball and football together," Johnny Valiant remembers. "He was also a pretty good amateur wrestler. Vince was definitely one of the guys, but he stood out. He was very self-assured. He was a leader, never a follower."

After graduation, Sullivan began considering a career in wrestling. It happened that WWWF Heavyweight Champion Bruno Sammartino was a resident of his native Pittsburgh, and so Sullivan literally knocked on the champ's door one day asking for help. Sammartino did indeed help get him started, and in 1969 he debuted in WWWF under the name John L. Sullivan—after the famous nineteenth-century boxing champion. In 1973, Sullivan ran into the man who would soon become his "brother," Jimmy Valiant, while both were competing in Ontario.

"Handsome" Jimmy Valiant had already had a memorable run in WWWF. Born James Valen in 1942 in Hammond, Indiana, he got started in the business at twenty-two after being spotted in the health club he worked in by former wrestlers who trained there. He initially changed his name to Jimmy Valentine, but this was changed in 1969 by Dallas promoter Fritz Von Erich to Jimmy Valiant, to avoid confusion with the already-established star Johnny Valentine.

Things picked up for Valiant when he was brought into WWWF in 1971 as the Tag Team partner of the ever-popular Chief Jay Strongbow. He sealed the deal by turning on Strongbow before the year was out, instantly placing himself among the nation's most hated ring villains.

Jimmy was so impressed with Sullivan that he offered to make him his Tag Team partner in the Indianapolis-based WWA, where he was competing at the time. John L. Sullivan became "Luscious" Johnny Valiant, bleaching his hair blond like his "brother" and taking on the same obnoxious attitude. They won the WWA Tag Team title in 1974, beating the formidable team of Sammartino & Dick the Bruiser.

They soon came to WWWF under the management of Capt.

Lou Albano and immediately took the World Tag Team title from Tony Garea & Dean Ho. They held that title for one year and five days, setting a record that would stand for fourteen years until being broken by Demolition in 1989. They elevated the Tag Team title to greater heights than it had ever known, engaging in a classic main event feud with Sammartino & Strongbow. The team of Dominic DeNucci & Victor Rivera brought their reign of terror to an end in May 1975.

"It was a successful time for us, and we were with each other every day," says Jimmy. "We got to know each other pretty well, and I always tell people that Johnny's still my brother."

After losing a match to Andre the Giant & AWA World Champion Verne Gagne at Madison Square Garden, the Valiants departed WWWF.

They returned in 1979, but when Jimmy contracted hepatitis,

Johnny had to bring in a third "brother." John Hill, who had previously wrestled as Guy Mitchell, debuted as "Gentleman" Jerry Valiant, and he and Johnny enjoyed a seven-month reign as Tag Team Champions. When Jimmy was well, he would join them and make it a three-man team, a precursor to such triads as the Fabulous Freebirds. The Valiants went their separate ways in 1980.

Shocked at the abundance of bleached-blond pretty boys in the game, Jimmy opted for an image overhaul, growing a long beard and becoming the unorthodox "Boogie Woogie Man." Throughout the 1980s, he would be a beloved fixture in southern territories like Memphis and the Carolinas.

Johnny made the shift to managing, beginning in the AWA with Hulk Hogan. By 1982 he was out of the business, a difficult divorce battle having taken its toll on his financial situation. But two years later, with *Hulkamania* raging in the World Wrestling Federation, Hogan would help get him back into the game.

"I was a single father, mopping floors on the graveyard shift at Westinghouse Electric in Pittsburgh," he recalls. "I was doing my kids' wash and making a meatloaf when Vince McMahon called me. Hogan's old friend Ed Leslie was coming in as Brutus Beefcake, and Hogan remembered me as a good speaker. So I followed my bliss and said, 'Count me in.' "

Shortening his name to Johnny V., the Luscious One remained a manager through the mid-1980s golden era of the Federation. He led Beefcake & Greg "The Hammer" Valentine—the Dream Team— to the Tag Team Championship, and ironically first brought Demolition to the Federation. After a three-year run, Johnny V. faded out of the managerial picture shortly after losing a Hair vs. Hair match to his former charge Beefcake.

In recent years, Jimmy Valiant has enjoyed training young athletes for the business in his two wrestling schools in Virginia and South Carolina. Luscious Johnny, meanwhile, can be found on the New York City comedy club scene, putting his gift of gab to good use.

The Valiant Brothers represented a crucial turning point in the history of Tag Team wrestling, an evolutionary step bridging earlier

- Blackjack Mulligan's daughter married wrestler Mike Rotundo, later known as Irwin R. Schyster.

- Blackjack Lanza discovered Diamond Dallas Page while Page was tending bar in Florida.

- In 1997, Mulligan's son Barry Windham and current WWE Superstar John "Bradshaw" Layfield teamed to become the New Blackjacks.

It seemed like they walked right out of a 1940s western, two sinister cowboys wearing black hats, black gloves, and black mustaches, with no respect for authority. Unlike most wrestling cowboys, usually known as benevolent characters, Blackjack Mulligan & Blackjack Lanza were cruel through and through, and left a trail of destruction in their wake, whether they were competing as a unit or individually.

The first to enter the sport was Lanza. Born October 14, 1935, in Albuquerque, New Mexico, John Lanza originally took as his vocation not wrestling but education. He studied to become a teacher, and spent two years teaching sociology.

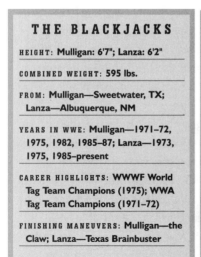

THE BLACKJACKS

HEIGHT: Mulligan: 6'7"; Lanza: 6'2"

COMBINED WEIGHT: 595 lbs.

FROM: Mulligan—Sweetwater, TX; Lanza—Albuquerque, NM

YEARS IN WWE: Mulligan—1971–72, 1975, 1982, 1985–87; Lanza—1973, 1975, 1985–present

CAREER HIGHLIGHTS: WWWF World Tag Team Champions (1975); WWA Tag Team Champions (1971–72)

FINISHING MANEUVERS: Mulligan—the Claw; Lanza—Texas Brainbuster

But in the mid-1960s his life took a change in course when he decided to become a professional wrestler. Taking advantage of his southwestern background, he dressed up in hat, boots, and vest and called himself "Cowboy" Jack Lanza. At first, he had a squeaky clean image that went along with the cowboy gimmick. But Lanza was just one of countless smiling cowpokes in the business.

His break came when he was brought into the Indianapolis-based WWA. His squeaky-clean image was jettisoned, and "Cowboy" Jack Lanza became the villainous Blackjack Lanza, taking on fledgling manager "Pretty Boy" Bobby Heenan as his mouthpiece. In 1967, he defeated Wilbur Snyder for the WWA Heavyweight crown, and held it twenty months before losing to Dick the Bruiser.

Lanza's persona was such a success that a young wrestler named Bob Windham thought it might bring him attention if he copied it. He was right. Born in 1941 in Sweetwater, Texas, Robert Windham grew up around the famous Funk family in nearby Amarillo. Dory Funk Sr. was then the area's top star, and Windham also knew of his two sons Dory Jr. and Terry, who would later become top-flight competitors in their own right.

Windham served in the marines in 1960, and was a member of the underwater demolition team while stationed in Guam. After returning home, he attended West Texas State, excelling in football. He was recruited by the New York Jets, but his promising career was derailed when he broke his leg. Sonny Werblin, head of the corporation that owned the Jets, was also CEO of the company that owned Madison Square Garden, and suggested that Windham try his hand at the wrestling game.

Originally billed under his given name, and soon after as Jack Mulligan, he got his start wrestling in the Midwest in 1969. He was wrestling and refereeing in Minneapolis when he was invited to come work for Vincent J. McMahon in the country's biggest territory, WWWF. Along the way, he adopted Lanza's "Blackjack" gimmick, making the leap from popular hero to despicable heel.

Blackjack Mulligan made his Madison Square Garden debut January 18, 1971, the night Ivan Koloff ended Bruno Sammartino's historic first reign as Heavyweight Champion. When the title quickly switched from Koloff to Pedro Morales, Mulligan became the next contender in line. In March, he challenged Morales in a hard-fought encounter at the Garden, but came up short. After losing a feud against the former champion Sammartino, Mulligan hightailed it out of WWWF.

As news spread of Mulligan's main-event attractions in the Northeast, it was obvious to team him with the originator, Lanza. The Blackjacks tag team was formed in the WWA, and with Bobby Heenan at their side, they captured the WWA Tag Team Championship in November 1971. They held it for eleven months before losing it to the famous team of the Crusher & Dick the Bruiser.

The team temporarily split up in 1973, when Blackjack Lanza came to the Northeast for his first run in WWWF. He formed a brief tag team with rookie Mike McCord—who would later achieve success in the South as Austin Idol—to challenge World Tag Team Champions Haystacks Calhoun & Tony Garea. He also warred with top WWWF Superstars Andre the Giant and Chief Jay Strongbow before rejoining Mulligan in Fritz Von Erich's World Class Championship Wrestling out of Dallas.

The Blackjacks finally made their way to WWWF as a team in the summer of 1975. Under the management of the illustrious Capt. Louis Albano, they won the World Tag Team Championship from Dominic DeNucci & "Irish" Pat Barrett in August. Their size and nasty demeanor grabbed a lot of attention during their relatively short reign, and they often found themselves competing against the likes of Andre the Giant, Gorilla Monsoon, and Ivan Putski. Former tag champs like DeNucci & Barrett and Garea & Dean Ho didn't stand a chance of regaining their title from the ornery cowboys.

That's why mat fans were caught by surprise when the unheralded duo of Tony Parisi & Louis Cerdan got the job done that November. Relieved of their title, the Blackjacks drifted out of WWWF. That would be the end of the Blackjacks Tag Team partnership. Having achieved the ultimate prize of the WWWF World

Tag Team title, they went their separate ways, looking for success on their own.

Blackjack Mulligan headed to the Carolinas, the NWA's premier territory. He became a fixture there, winning the U.S. title three times between 1976 and 1978, and tangling with the likes of Bobo Brazil, Mr. Wrestling, and a rookie Rick Steamboat. In August 1979, he spent two weeks as half of the NWA World Tag Team Champions, along with another young whippersnapper named Ric Flair.

In 1982 he returned to World Wrestling Federation, waging a full-scale war with fellow behemoth Andre the Giant and taking a crack at Bob Backlund's Heavyweight title.

After the Blackjacks breakup, Lanza headed to the AWA, where he once again came under the management of close friend Bobby Heenan. He formed the second great tag team of his career, with Bobby Duncum Sr., and won the AWA World Tag Team Championship from Crusher & Bruiser in July 1976. Lanza & Duncum were World Champions for a year before being dethroned by Greg Gagne & Jumpin' Jim Brunzell, the High Flyers.

Lanza spent most of the next few years in the AWA. By 1984, Mulligan had found his way there, and the duo reunited for one last hurrah. At this point in their careers, they had both been accepted into the fans' good graces, and so the Blackjacks reunion was hailed throughout the Midwest.

But it wouldn't last long. In the Northeast, World Wrestling Federation was riding high on the shoulders of Heavyweight Champion Hulk Hogan and promoter Vincent K. McMahon, who had taken over from his ailing father. They were spreading nationwide, and the AWA was hit badly by the expansion. Both Mulligan and Lanza joined the stream of New York–bound talent, although in different capacities. While Mulligan was hired as an active wrestler, Lanza ended his wrestling career and joined the Federation as a backstage road agent.

"I liked what I saw going on," he says. "I always say that Vince took a business that had been stagnant for fifty years, opened the window, and let fresh air into the room."

During his final Federation run, Blackjack Mulligan finally heard the cheers of fans instead of hissing and boos. In addition to competing under his established name, he also donned a mask and took part in an unorthodox tag team called the Machines. Known as Big Machine, he was joined by Super Machine (Bill Eadie, aka Demolition Axe) and even Giant Machine (who everyone could clearly tell was Andre the Giant). Over the summer of 1986, the Machines made life miserable for Bobby Heenan and his stable.

Mulligan left at the beginning of 1987, competing three more years before finally retiring. Calling on the skills he learned in the marines, he pursued deep-sea diving as a full-time hobby. To this day, the man once known as Blackjack Mulligan enjoys exploring underwater caves and shipwrecks, as well as getting some relief from the trials of lugging his 300-plus-pound battle-worn body around on dry land.

Lanza, meanwhile, became a respected fixture of WWE's road agent crew, and remains so today.

"Every night's a different challenge," he says. "Planes are running late. Superstars get hurt. People have family problems. You have to be a trainer, a psychologist, and a father figure."

But Jack Lanza wouldn't trade it for anything—certainly not to have his wrestling career back. "I like being retired," he says. "When I go places, nobody bothers me. I can walk through airports and be anonymous. I don't think about things I did twenty-five, thirty years ago. I get my kicks from being creative and seeing other guys in the spotlight."

Indeed, the days of the Blackjacks rampaging through territories like Old West desperadoes may be long gone, but both remain vital. Lanza in particular has been a trusted member of the WWE family for more than twenty years.

- Afa & Sika are related to heavyweight boxer David Tua.

- The Samoans have held a record twenty-two Tag Team championships around the world.

- Among the graduates of Afa's Wild Samoan Training Center are Billy Kidman and Batista.

It's a tiny chain of islands in the South Pacific at latitude 15 south, longitude 170 west, right on the international date line. Yet diminutive as it may appear on a globe, Samoa looms large in the world of professional wrestling. Over the past three decades, it has produced a veritable legion of ring competitors, most notably, the extended Anoa'i family. Foremost among this family were the Wild Samoans, Afa & Sika, a brother Tag Team that terrorized the sport for more than a dozen years.

Afa & Sika were born Alofa and Leati Anoa'i, respectively, two of the eleven children of the Reverend Amituanai Anoa'i and his wife, Tovale. They grew up in American Samoa, the portion of the islands that is a territory of the United States. There, they learned an appreciation for wrestling from an early age.

THE WILD SAMOANS

HEIGHT: Afa: 6'1"; Sika: 6'2"

COMBINED WEIGHT: 624 lbs.

FROM: Samoa

YEARS IN WWE: Afa—1980, 1983–84, 1992–94; Sika—1980, 1983–84, 1986–88

CAREER HIGHLIGHTS: 3-time World Wrestling Federation Tag Team Champions (1980, 1980, 1983)

FINISHING MANEUVER: Top rope splash

"Every Samoan is a wrestling fan," says Sika. "When wrestling comes on, everything stops. Wrestling comes first in Samoa, then church."

When the family relocated to San Francisco, they fit in well with the city's sizable Samoan population. Alofa and Leati became fans of one of the area's top wrestling stars, the Samoan-born High Chief Peter Maivia.

Alofa was the first to actually enter the sport. After serving in the marines as a teenager, he started training with Maivia and the High Chief's son-in-law, Rocky Johnson. Traveling to Arizona with a friend who was trying to break into wrestling there, Alofa wound up getting hired by the promoters, who were impressed with his looks and abilities.

He immediately set about training his younger brother Leati, with the idea that they could compete as a Tag Team. In 1973 they debuted in Stu Hart's Stampede Wrestling out of Calgary. Known as Afa & Sika, they were at first presented as sympathetic characters, much like Maivia and other "happy-go-lucky" island competitors. But that didn't last.

"We were too rough," explains Sika. "It was hard for people to feel sorry for us. So we went the other way."

Capitalizing on the stereotypes that surrounded people of their heritage, Afa & Sika became the Wild Samoans, uncontrollable savages who spoke only Samoan. With overgrown hair and traditional sarongs, they wrestled barefoot and often munched on raw fish. Their style was completely unorthodox, and gained instant attention from fans who were both fascinated and revolted by them.

"We acted crazy because we *were* crazy," laughs Afa. "And the people believed it because it was real."

After dominating Canada and much of the American South over the course of the 1970s, they appeared in World Wrestling Federation under the management of Capt. Lou Albano at the beginning of 1980. They made big waves right off the bat, winning the World Tag Team title from Tito Santana & Ivan Putski in April and taking their shot individually at Bob Backlund's Heavyweight

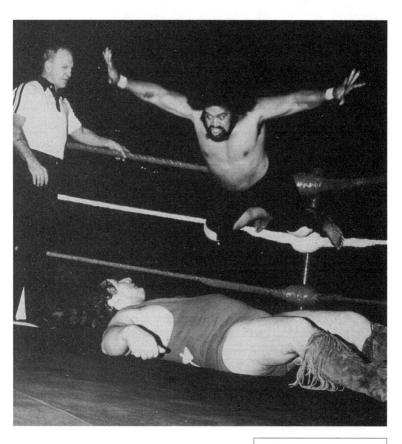

Championship. They lost their title to Backlund and Pedro Morales as part of a mega-event held in Shea Stadium in August.

Yet Backlund & Morales were forced to give up the gold due to the Federation's restrictions on Superstars holding more than one title simultaneously. And when the vacant championship went up for grabs in a tournament, it was the tenacious Samoans who recaptured it, beating Tony Garea & Rene Goulet in the finals. Garea would regroup two months later with a new partner, Rick Martel, and relieve Afa & Sika of the title once again.

They departed the Federation, spending much of the next two years in Georgia Championship Wrestling. At the start of 1983, they were back on the scene, soon adding a third member to the team, Afa's son Samu. In March, they beat the Strongbows for their third Federation Tag Team title, becoming only the second team to accomplish such a feat. They would go on to enjoy their longest reign, holding the titles for eight months.

The Samoans left the Federation for the last time as a team in late 1984, and spent the next couple of years in Bill Watts's Mid-South Championship Wrestling before splitting up in 1986. Afa established a wrestling school, first in Connecticut, and then in Allentown, Pennsylvania, where he opened up the Wild Samoan Training Center. Sika continued a little longer as an active competitor, spending a year and a half back in World Wrestling Federation, where he often teamed with Kamala the Ugandan Giant.

Afa would also return to the Federation for a couple of years in the early 1990s, as the manager of a new team of Samoans, the Headshrinkers, composed of his son Samu and nephew Fatu (better known as Rikishi).

Today, Afa runs not only his training center but also a local promotion called World X-Treme Wrestling (WXW). Both he and Sika are actively involved in a number of charities as well.

Their family includes not only Samu and Rikishi, but nephews Jamal, the Tonga Kid, and the late Yokozuna, as well as Sika's son Matthew, known today in WWE as Rosey. Add to that their extended Samoan "family," which includes Maivia, Johnson, The Rock, and Jimmy Snuka, and you have the most closely knit unit anywhere in the business. And at the heart of it all are the two brothers who comprised one of the longest running Tag Teams in history.

- Tony's father, Ivan Gareljich, hailed from Podgora, Croatia.

- On June 8, 1981, Garea beat a young rookie named Chris Canyon in Madison Square Garden. Four years later, Canyon would return as King Kong Bundy.

- Out of thirty-five years in the business, Garea has spent thirty-two in WWE.

During WWE's early years as a northeastern wrestling territory, most performers came and went, spreading their time out among the many promotions that covered North America in those days. Yet there were some individuals, like Gorilla Monsoon and Bruno Sammartino, who made the region pretty much their permanent home. Another of those individuals is Tony Garea, who has been with the company for the better part of three decades. He's shown unparalleled loyalty and dedication throughout a career that can be divided almost in half between his years as a popular wrestler and as a trusted road agent.

He was born Anthony Gareljich on September 20, 1946, in Auckland, New Zealand, the son of parents of Yugoslavian and Irish descent. As a youth, he played rugby and enjoyed weight

---

TONY GAREA

HEIGHT: 6'1"

WEIGHT: 245 lbs.

FROM: Auckland, New Zealand

YEARS IN WWE: 1972–75; 1977–79; 1980–present

CAREER HIGHLIGHTS: 1972 Rookie of the Year; 5-time World Tag Team Champion (1973, 1973, 1978, 1980, 1981)

FINISHING MANEUVER: Abdominal stretch

training, which very quickly gave him a muscular physique that would later be to his great advantage.

In 1971, he made his wrestling debut in his native New Zealand. His reasons started out pragmatic, but things soon changed. "I did it for a little extra cash," he admits. "Then, it became a way of life."

After leaving New Zealand, Garea first headed to nearby Australia, then made the big move to the United States. He spent the remainder of his first year competing in Florida for promoter Eddie Graham. In his wrestling days, Graham had been a Tag Team Champion for Northeast promoter Vincent J. McMahon, and maintained a rapport with his now fellow promoter. When McMahon was looking for a fresh young "babyface" hero for his World Wide Wrestling Federation, Graham told him he had just the guy.

Garea made his first WWWF appearance at a TV taping in the Philadelphia Arena on September 20, 1972, defeating Davey O'Hannon. After completing three tapings, Garea returned to Florida, but was called back just three weeks later for another round of tapings. Next up was his first live WWWF arena event, in Patterson, New Jersey, on October 27. Exactly one month later, he was appearing on the undercard at Madison Square Garden in a match that saw him beat John Minton, the rookie who would later become Big John Studd.

Garea became a sensation in his new home, gaining popularity through his good looks and repertoire of aerial moves that were quite exciting for that era. Female fans turned him into a heartthrob, and they were well represented in the fan vote that named him 1972 WWWF Rookie of the Year.

"It really amazed me," he recollects. "From the moment I went out that first time, I got quite an ovation. People were comparing me to Jack Brisco. Something just clicked. You either have it or you don't. And nobody knows exactly what *it* is."

In May 1973, Garea began what would be an amazing run in the WWWF's Tag Team division when he joined forces with the 601-pound veteran Haystacks Calhoun. Garea & Calhoun toppled

Mr. Fuji & Professor Toru Tanaka for the World Tag Team Championship in Hamburg, Pennsylvania, and would hold on to the title through the summer of '73. Fuji & Tanaka eventually took it back, but that was just the beginning of Garea's Tag Team accomplishments.

By the end of the year, Garea had formed another successful alliance with the "Happy Hawaiian" Dean Ho, who had previously beaten both Fuji and Tanaka in singles competition. Sure enough, Garea & Ho relieved the Japanese duo of their belts in November of 1973. A six-month title reign ensued. In May of 1974, Capt. Lou Albano's newest combination, Jimmy & Johnny Valiant, defeated Garea & Ho in Hamburg. The ex-champs tried to regain their gold, but the Valiant Brothers would hold the title for over a year.

After suffering some setbacks both in his alliance with Ho and his singles pursuits, Garea saw fit to end his first WWWF stint and try his hand at some other territories. He spent the second half of 1975 in Jim Barnett's Georgia Championship Wrestling, and then headed out to Roy Shire's San Francisco promotion for the following year. While there, he enjoyed a run as NWA World Tag Team Champion with the area's top headliner, Pat Patterson.

Garea returned to WWWF in 1977 and formed a new tandem with another young Superstar, Bruno Sammartino's protégé Larry Zbysko. They were consistent challengers to World Tag Team Champions Mr. Fuji & Prof. Toru Tanaka, but were unable to win the title at that time. But even bigger than the Tag Team title picture, Garea was in consideration at the time to be WWWF's next top titleholder. The hated Superstar Billy Graham had dethroned Sammartino as Heavyweight Champion, and Garea's name was on the list of those being considered to replace Bruno as the next company flagbearer.

"I was a little nervous when I heard the rumors," he remembers. "I wasn't sure if I could carry the championship. I felt it to be a big responsibility."

In the end, Bob Backlund wound up beating Graham and taking on that coveted position, so Garea renewed his focus on the alliance with Zbysko. The duo captured the Tag Team title from the Yukon Lumberjacks on November 21, 1978.

Just four weeks later, while still coholder of WWWF Tag Team title, Garea was picked to be part of wrestling history at Madison Square Garden. For the first time in sixteen years, the NWA World Heavyweight Championship, then held by Harley Race, would be defended within WWWF territory. Garea was Race's challenger, and fought gallantly against the champion before losing a hard-fought match.

In March 1979, Garea & Zbysko dropped their gold to the newest Valiant Brothers combination, "Luscious" Johnny & "Gentleman" Jerry. Garea departed the area and headed to Jim Crockett's Mid-Atlantic Championship Wrestling, then the NWA's most high-profile promotion. He spent a year there before returning to McMahon-land in the summer of 1980. He hasn't stopped working there since.

The first thing he noticed upon his return was the dramatic transformation of his once squeaky-clean partner Zbysko. Larry had turned on his mentor Sammartino and become one of the most despised figures in the sport. Garea quickly found himself embroiled in a feud with his onetime ally, in which no clear winner was ever truly decided.

Returning to what he knew best, Tag Team competition, Garea set his sights on yet another new and promising talent, the French-Canadian Rick Martel. This alliance would prove the most fruitful of all of them. On November 8, 1980, they bested Lou Albano's Wild Samoans, Afa & Sika, for the World Tag Team title. They were immediately challenged by another Albano duo, the unorthodox Moondogs, who hounded them for months. Finally in March, they were successful in beating the champs.

But just four months later, the extremely popular Garea & Martel accomplished something none of Garea's previous partnerships had been able to do—they regained the gold. In doing so, Garea became a five-time World Wrestling Federation Tag Team Champion, setting a record that would stand for seventeen years before being broken by Billy Gunn in 1998.

The team enjoyed three more months at the top of the division, before losing a highly controversial bout to Mr. Fuji & Mr. Saito. Martel was pinned after having salt thrown in his eyes by Fuji, but since the ref missed it, the title change stood.

Garea & Martel remained together for another half a year, but they never could get back to the top. Garea began to settle into the lower mid-card, consistently beating midlevel competitors like Steve Travis and Johnny Rodz, and forming temporary teams with other popular stars like Rocky Johnson, Curt Hennig, and Eddie Gilbert. Then, he started finding himself on the losing end against competitors who were using him as a stepping-stone to bigger things, like Ray "The Crippler" Stevens and the Iron Sheik.

After Hulk Hogan became Heavyweight Champion in 1984, a new era began in World Wrestling Federation. Garea remained a part of the active roster for the first few years of that new era, but he never again reached the prominence he once had. He lingered until 1987, when he decided to walk away from the business to return to New Zealand to join his brother doing construction work. Before he could do so, he was offered a new job with World Wrestling Federation, that of a road agent.

"From the beginning, I enjoyed it," Garea says. "The guys were my friends, so they trusted me. And I did everything to keep that trust. I gave them all the advice I could."

For the past nineteen years, Tony Garea has remained a WWE mainstay in his road agent capacity. Coordinating activities backstage and imparting his wisdom to the Superstars, he is a constant fixture in the locker room on almost any given night. With his presence, he provides a direct link from the global WWE of today to the territorial WWWF of yesteryear.

"I've never grown tired of this business," he says. "I enjoyed it thirty years ago. I enjoyed it fifteen years ago. And I enjoy it today."

- Early in his career, Pat Patterson had the nickname "Killer."
- Patterson refereed the main event of the very first *WrestleMania*.
- Among his many creative contributions was the concept of the *Royal Rumble* match, which he came up with in the late 1980s.

Like "Classy" Freddie Blassie years before him, Pat Patterson was a West Coast headliner who came to work for the McMahons toward the end of his in-ring career, and went on to become one of WWE's most loyal and respected employees. For a quarter of a century, Patterson was an indispensable part of the company. A trusted adviser to Vince McMahon, Patterson was present during the company's critical expansion era of the mid-1980s. His creative input and knowledge of wrestling psychology has been a mainstay of the WWE product.

He was born Pierre Clermont in Montreal, Quebec, on January 19, 1941. His Roman Catholic upbringing made him a deeply reli-

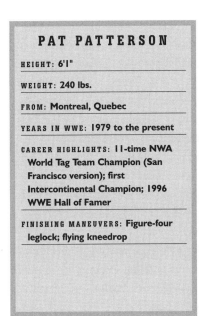

PAT PATTERSON

HEIGHT: 6'1"

WEIGHT: 240 lbs.

FROM: Montreal, Quebec

YEARS IN WWE: 1979 to the present

CAREER HIGHLIGHTS: 11-time NWA World Tag Team Champion (San Francisco version); first Intercontinental Champion; 1996 WWE Hall of Famer

FINISHING MANEUVERS: Figure-four leglock; flying kneedrop

gious child, and he served as an altar boy while attending school. As a teenager, he showed an interest in the priesthood, but was advised that it simply wasn't his vocation.

"I went to my priest and spoke to him about it," he recalls. "They were looking for candidates. But they weren't interested in me. [They told me,] 'It won't work. You're too adventurous.' And so I started looking for something else to do with my life."

After learning he was not cut out for the cloth, Clermont looked for a career more in tune with his "adventurous" nature. As a teenager, he took a liking to the wrestling matches that were put on in his hometown, and started asking around about how he might break into that exciting business, confident that his background in gymnastics would give him an advantage.

Before long, Clermont was training under Montreal regular Pat Girard. As was the custom of the day, the veteran trainers tortured the young Clermont with painful holds and punishing amateur moves, trying to see if he really had the determination to continue. Once they realized he was serious, they groomed him for a professional career.

He debuted in Montreal in 1958, at seventeen. Hoping to appeal to fans outside the local French Canadian community, Clermont sought out an "Anglo-sized" wrestling name, settling on the generic-sounding "Pat Patterson." Right from the start, he knew wrestling was the life for him.

"My friends and family never came to my matches," Patterson recalls. "They thought I was making a mistake, taking home just five to ten dollars a night to get my brains beat out. But I loved the excitement, getting the people riled up, controlling their reactions to everything I did. I loved being an entertainer."

In the early 1960s, without any English and with roughly fifty dollars in his pocket, Patterson took his act to America for the first time. He first competed in the NWA's Pacific Northwest territory. Looking to give the young wrestler a little more color, a promoter in Washington helped him come up with an effeminate "pretty boy" persona, complete with beret, cigarette holder, and lipstick. Soon Patterson was making his way up the ranks.

It was when the twenty-four-year-old Patterson headed south to San Francisco that his star really began to rise. Almost overnight, he became one of the top drawing cards for promoter Roy Shire's West Coast promotion. Between 1965 and 1977, he won Frisco's version of the NWA World Tag Team title (the original one) eleven times with eight different partners. Among them were future WWWF Heavyweight Champion Superstar Billy Graham, former WWWF Heavyweight Champion Pedro Morales, and Tony Garea. He also teamed with both The Rock's father, Rocky Johnson, and grandfather, High Chief Peter Maivia.

But his pairing with the late Ray "The Crippler" Stevens would be remembered above them all. Patterson & Stevens became San Francisco favorites. Their renown eventually reached such a peak that they were able to tour other territories together. In 1978, they won the AWA World Tag Team title, becoming the first duo to win World titles in both the NWA and AWA.

Between 1969 and 1977, Patterson held the area's top prize, the NWA U.S. title, six times. During this period, he was Roy Shire's number-one attraction. He also began to show what a keen mind for the inner workings of the business he truly had. Shire made him his right-hand man behind the scenes, giving Patterson the responsibility of running shows that he couldn't attend, and involving him in matchmaking.

"In those days, you couldn't stay in a territory for more than two or three years," says Patterson. "[But] I was a regular in the Bay Area for sixteen years. The way I kept myself fresh was to keep changing my character. Sometimes I was a babyface, then I was a heel. The point was making the fans care, and I think we did a pretty good job."

Among his peers, Patterson came to be regarded as a leader, a ring general. He was a quick learner, gifted with the ability to absorb as much knowledge about the business as was given to him, and during his time with Shire he truly blossomed into a first-rate performer and matchmaker. He earned a reputation as a great communicator who cared a lot about those who worked with him.

Patterson won the famous San Francisco Cow Palace Battle

Royal in 1975. Just two years later, the Shire promotion was in a decline. Seeking opportunities elsewhere, Patterson spent time wrestling in Los Angeles and Florida. In the summer of 1979, he made his way to World Wrestling Federation for the very first time.

Banking on Patterson's West Coast notoriety, Vincent J. McMahon immediately matched him up against Heavyweight Champion Bob Backlund in Madison Square Garden. Over a twelve-week period, the two would meet on four consecutive occasions at the arena—a Garden record that still stands. Patterson won two of the first three by count-out, and battled with Backlund to a double count-out in the third. In their fourth and final encounter, the champ bested the French Canadian in a Steel Cage match.

The series against Backlund made Pat Patterson into an instant East Coast superstar. He had already won the brand-new World Wrestling Federation North American Championship from a young Ted DiBiase in June, but after his tremendous showing against Backlund, the title was upgraded to the Intercontinental Championship—a reflection of the prestige Patterson brought to it.

At the start of 1980, Patterson had a falling-out with his villainous manager, Capt. Lou Albano, that turned him into a Federation fan favorite. The first Intercontinental Champion was experiencing cheers for the first time since joining the company. On April 21, his inaugural Intercontinental title reign was brought to an end by Olympic strongman Ken Patera, and the two would battle throughout the summer of '80 as Patterson made a vain attempt to get it back.

The spring of 1981 found Patterson embroiled in his most famous Federation feud of all, against Sgt. Slaughter. Their Alley Fight at Madison Square Garden is still talked about as one of the greatest bouts in Federation history, and was exceedingly brutal for its time. Also that year, Patterson made a brief return to his old SF stomping grounds, winning the Cow Palace Battle Royal one last time before the Shire promotion lowered its curtain for good.

Patterson's in-ring career was winding down by 1982, but that certainly didn't mean he was ready to leave the business. Vincent

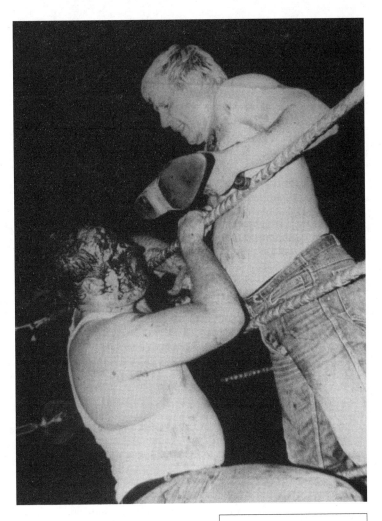

Sgt. Slaughter vs. Pat Patterson.

K. McMahon was in the process of taking over from his father, change was in the air, and Patterson was diversifying. He became a TV announcer, calling the action alongside McMahon with his thick Quebecois accent.

"It just proves that if you want to do something badly enough in this business, you can do it," says Patterson. "I couldn't even speak English, and I was a color commentator. Vince would rib me—asking me questions with complicated words I didn't understand—but I managed to get away with it."

His position in the company was evolving. As the Federation expanded across the nation and professional wrestling redefined itself, Patterson was right there in the middle of it. Drawing on his experience as Roy Shire's top adviser, he took on that role with Vince McMahon, becoming the Federation's chief matchmaker and creative architect.

For the rest of the 1980s and into the '90s, Patterson helped guide the course of Federation TV from behind the scenes. He developed many new and innovative ideas, and helped prepare rising Superstars for the limelight.

During the company's "Attitude" era of the late 1990s, Patterson once again enjoyed an on-air role. In a spoof of his actual job, Patterson played the part of one of the evil Mr. McMahon's flunkies, or "stooges." The comedy duo he formed with fellow stooge Jerry Brisco during that period delivered some truly hilarious moments.

"I've given my life to wrestling, and I like to think I've helped a lot of people in it," he says. "Some appreciate it. Some don't. But that's all part of the business."

In November 2004, after years of contemplating retirement, Patterson finally called it a career. His official last day was the first *Taboo Tuesday* Pay-Per-View event, after which he was given an emotional tribute in the ring that included him singing his own rendition of Frank Sinatra's "My Way." From time to time, he still appears backstage to contribute ideas, most notably at *WrestleMania 21*—proving that he will always be an integral part of WWE.

- Ken's brother Jack Patera was the head coach of the NFL's Seattle Seahawks from 1976 to 1982.
- Patera was the first man to press 500 pounds.
- Ric Flair's father, an ob-gyn, was partners with the doctor who delivered both of Patera's children.

There have been strongmen in WWE over the years, men who shocked and amazed fans with their sheer power. And then there was Ken Patera.

He was born November 6, 1942, in Portland, Oregon. Although he would first take a detour through the world of weightlifting, he had his eye on professional wrestling from the start.

"I always wanted to do it," he says. "The only sport on TV when I was growing up, back in '53 when we got our first TV, was wrestling. The wrestling down at the old armory in downtown

KEN PATERA

HEIGHT: 6'1"

WEIGHT: 275 lbs.

FROM: Portland, OR

YEARS IN WWE: 1977–80; 1984–85; 1987–88

CAREER HIGHLIGHTS: Intercontinental Champion (1980); 2-time AWA World Tag Team Champion (1983, w/Jerry Blackwell, 1989, w/Brad Rheingans); 1972 Olympic weightlifter; 4-time gold medalist, 1971 Pan Am Games

FINISHING MANEUVER: Swinging neck-breaker (aka swinging full nelson)

NICKNAME: The Olympic Strongman

Portland. They had about four hundred people at the most. I was kind of intrigued and used to go to the shows once in a while."

His athletic career began in earnest at Brigham Young University in the 1960s. While there, he placed third in an NCAA shot-put tournament, and as a powerlifter bench-pressed 560 pounds, squatted 820 pounds, and deadlifted 785 pounds. While Patera's three brothers played college football, and he played in high school, team sports did not hold his interest. While still in school, he became acquainted with wrestlers Billy White Wolf and Herb Freeman, who taught him how to lift weights.

In 1970, while he was preparing for the Pan American Games, his brother Jack, then the defensive coach for the Minnesota Vikings, introduced him to Verne Gagne, owner of the Minneapolis-based American Wrestling Association (AWA). Patera expressed his intention of competing in the Pan Am Games (where he won four gold medals) and the Olympics the following year, and the two came to the agreement that Patera would come to work for the AWA afterward.

Patera got closer and closer to the business in the early 1970s, at one point even living with a young Ric Flair right before he broke into the game himself. Those were wild times, in which Patera came to be known as a guy who would frequently keep the party going all night long. Yet as much of a partier as he was, he was also vehemently dedicated to his training regimen. Once the Olympics were over, he was ready for Gagne's training camp. Or at least he thought he was.

"It was in one of his horse barns," Patera remembers. "There was one light on. The horses were downstairs and the chickens were upstairs on the right. The slats in the barn were about an inch apart, and there were times when we would show up and there would be four-foot snowdrifts inside the barn. The chickens would be up roosting on the crossbeams of the barn, shitting on the ring. We'd have to clean the mat down. The ring was all broken down, big holes in it. The ropes were all fucked up, they weren't tight at all. Here's a guy who was a multimillionaire, and he had the worst possible conditions for us to train in. It was bizarre."

Ken Patera vs. Dusty Rhodes.

The camp was run by American Wrestling Association owner Verne Gagne, and it was in the AWA that Patera debuted in 1973, wrestling his first match against George "Scrap Iron" Gadaski (the same man Flair faced in his first match). His fame as an Olympic weightlifter preceded him, but he also had a natural charisma that made him a perfect fit for the wrestling ring and created such a reputation that his Olympic background was more a bonus than a defining factor. The feats of strength he regularly performed were just as engaging as what he could do between the ropes.

The massive muscleman first appeared in WWWF four years after his pro debut, and gave then–Heavyweight Champion Bruno Sammartino some of the toughest challenges of his second title reign. Patera was one of the most hated men on the roster; the ultimate bully who was never above taking advantage of his imposing size and strength to get what he wanted. His swinging neckbreaker, a crippling variation on the full nelson, was one of the most feared submission holds in the sport, and shortened the careers of many an opponent.

In April 1980, Patera defeated Pat Patterson to become the second Intercontinental Champion. He held the title for most of the year, and his reign included a defense against Tony Atlas at Shea Stadium, a true battle of strongmen.

After losing the title to Pedro Morales, Patera continued to be a dominating force in World Wrestling Federation, first under the management of the Grand Wizard, and later Bobby "The Brain" Heenan. His 1980 Texas Death match against Bob Backlund is remembered as a classic. He helped Big John Studd to "rape Andre the Giant of his dignity" by cutting the trademark hair of the Eighth Wonder of the World in 1984.

Patera returned to the AWA in the early 1980s, and held the World Tag Team title for close to a year with "Crusher" Jerry Blackwell. Shortly after that, he found himself behind bars thanks to an incident in Wisconsin in which he and fellow wrestler Masa Saito first hurled a boulder through the window of a McDonald's that refused to serve them after hours, and then brawled with police who arrived on the scene. Even Patera's awesome might was not enough to beat the judicial system, and he was sentenced to two years in prison. He served his time with honor and dignity, paying his debt to society and returning to the Federation in 1987.

This time, Patera was beloved by fans due in part to the admirable way he had handled his prison experience. But former manager Heenan wouldn't let sleeping dogs lie, and he goaded the Olympian into the last great feud of his career, an ongoing war with the Bobby Heenan stable that lasted well into the following year. During that time, Patera also took part in the first *Survivor Series* and the Heavyweight Championship tournament at *WrestleMania IV*, as well as the first *SummerSlam*.

After departing the World Wrestling Federation a final time, Patera returned in 1989 to the AWA, then in the midst of collapse. He continued with the organization until its demise at the start of 1991, and then competed sporadically for midwestern independents for the next several years. These days, he resides in Minneapolis, running his own training facility in nearby Prescott, Wisconsin, as well as his own promotion, the World All-Star Wrestling Alliance (WAWA).

Remembered for his brute strength and brawny physique, Ken Patera was a perennial highlight of World Wrestling Federation programming during much of the 1970s and '80s.

- Muraco won the first *King of the Ring* tournament in 1985—eight years before it became an annual Pay-Per-View.

- The Grand Wizard is the godfather of Muraco's daughter.

- The Magnificent One defeated an opponent once while eating a sandwich!

For an entire generation of World Wrestling Federation fans of the early 1980s, there is a man who stands out as among the most memorable. Ask anyone watching during that era, and almost without fail one of the first names on their lips will be: the Magnificent Muraco. His intensity, charisma, and work ethic in the ring made him unforgettable, and even though crowds showered him with disdain, it was that certain kind of disdain unique to the wrestling business that is perhaps the greatest show of appreciation.

He was born Don Morrow on September 10, 1949, in Sunset Beach, Hawai'i. The Pacific island chain was a common stopover for American wrestlers on their way to Australia and Japan, and the young Morrow gained an interest in the sport from an early age by attending local shows. He wrestled for Punahou High School, winning championships in his junior and senior years.

THE MAGNIFICENT MURACO

HEIGHT: 6'4"

WEIGHT: 274 lbs.

FROM: Sunset Beach, Hawaii

YEARS IN WWE: 1980–88

CAREER HIGHLIGHTS: 2-time Intercontinental Champion (1981; 1983–84); 2004 WWE Hall of Famer

FINISHING MANEUVERS: Reverse piledriver; Asian spike

NICKNAMES: The Magnificent One; Beach Bum; The Rock

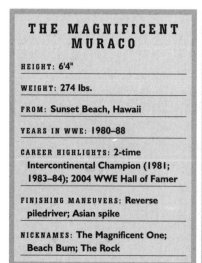

Morrow had a passion for surfing, and after graduation he competed in a surfing contest with the son of British wrestling legend Lord James Blears, then a Hawai'i resident. When Blears met the youngster, he realized he'd be a natural for wrestling, and took him under his wing. In 1970, he sent Morrow to Vancouver to train for the ring.

In the 1970s, Don Morrow became Don Muraco. Tall, dark, and handsome, he started as a matinee-idol-style fan favorite, but his cocky demeanor eventually got the better of him, and he took to calling himself the Magnificent Muraco. He went about the business of making a name for himself, traveling to many different regions. In Los Angeles, he held the NWA Americas Championship; in San Francisco he was NWA U.S. Champion; and in Tampa he captured the NWA Florida Championship.

In contrast to his in-ring demeanor, behind the scenes Don Muraco was a laid-back, easygoing individual, whom few can recall ever seeing upset. Nevertheless, in the ring, he knew how to feel out an audience and respond, provoking just the kind of responses he was looking for.

The Magnificent One signed with World Wrestling Federation in late 1980 to begin the run that would be the centerpiece of his career.

"It was one of the places everybody wanted to be," he says, "because you were wrestling in big arenas, where you made more money."

Managed by the Grand Wizard, he immediately grabbed attention with his gruff interview style and the despicably arrogant way in which he carried himself. Aware of his Hawai'ian origin, fans taunted him with chants of "beach bum." But the hate only fueled his success. In June 1981 he dethroned Pedro Morales for the Intercontinental Championship and jumped to the number-one contender's position, engaging Heavyweight Champion Bob Backlund in a series of encounters, several of which were sixty-minute draws.

"[Backlund] represented professional wrestling, and he took it seriously," he says. "I had a lot of respect for him. Once, we wres-

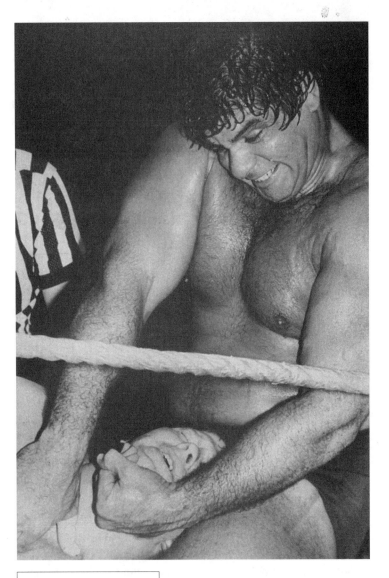

Don Muraco vs. Bob Backlund.

tled each other at the Capital Centre in Maryland for an hour in the afternoon, then drove to Philadelphia and had an entirely different match for another hour."

Muraco lost the Intercontinental title back to Morales at Madison Square Garden in November, part of the bloody war that raged between the two for nearly two years. After disappearing for several months, he returned at the end of 1982 to again engage Pedro for the Intercontinental gold. In January 1983, he finally regained the prize, this time holding it in his possession for a full year.

After making another run at Backlund, Muraco defended the Intercontinental title against tough contenders like Rocky Johnson. But his toughest challenger would be Jimmy "Superfly" Snuka, against whom Muraco would have his most famous match. The encounter at the Garden on October 17, 1983, is remembered not so much for Muraco's victory as for the Superfly's majestic leap after the match was over.

"We were selling out everywhere, so we had this Cage match," Muraco says. "Everybody wanted to see Snuka go off the top of the cage and beat me for the title. The fans were mad [when] I escaped and managed to keep my title. So Snuka dragged me back in, climbed up to the top of the cage, and did his Superfly leap onto me. The fans went wild, and I really got hurt."

In February 1984, the Magnificent One was at last unseated for good as Intercontinental Champion by Tito Santana in Boston. The Hawai'ian took another sabbatical, but when he returned the following year, he was right back at the top as number-one contender to the Heavyweight Championship, at that time held by Hulk Hogan. On the heels of the first *WrestleMania*, Muraco opposed the Hulkster in his last great main-event run.

For a time in 1987, Muraco and "Cowboy" Bob Orton had a regular Tag Team partnership, the breakup of which would lead to Muraco finally abandoning his evil ways and embracing the fans for the first time in his Federation career. Clad in tie-dye and managed by Superstar Billy Graham, he became known as "The Rock" Don Muraco.

"I didn't like being cheered," he says. "I'd been a heel for so long; it didn't feel right any other way."

Muraco's babyface run was short-lived. After participating in the first *Survivor Series* in November 1987, the Heavyweight Championship tournament at *WrestleMania IV*, and the first

SummerSlam in August 1988, the original "Rock" disappeared from the Federation for good.

Into the 1990s and beyond, the ultra-charismatic Muraco has maintained his ties to the business. He inducted old foe Jimmy Snuka into the WWE Hall of Fame in 1996, and last year helped establish Hawai'i Championship Wrestling, the island state's first major promotion in fifteen years. His years in the ring may be over, but he remains involved in the business in which he excelled.

- Calhoun inspired a number of later imitators, including Haystacks Muldoon, the U.K.'s Giant Haystacks, and even Haystacks Calhoun Jr.

- Haystacks used to have a pet Chihuahua that slept with him in his bed—until the night he rolled over and squashed it!

- The only time Calhoun was ever outweighed was when he wrestled Happy Humphrey, who tipped the scales at 750 pounds—and is believed to have been the heaviest wrestler who ever lived.

There have been many giants in WWE. But before Yokozuna, before Andre, before Gorilla Monsoon, there was Haystacks Calhoun, the mammoth country boy from Morgan's Corner, Arkansas. Calhoun was a legend across America during the 1950s and '60s, and to this day his very name connotes great size and girth. Haystacks Calhoun was an oddity in a sport of oddities, and his presence was usually the highlight of any card.

William D. Calhoun was born in McKinney, Texas, on August 3, 1934. At the time of his birth, he weighed just 11 pounds. But

HAYSTACKS CALHOUN

HEIGHT: 6'4"

WEIGHT: 601 lbs.

FROM: Morgan's Corner, AR

YEARS IN WWE: 1958–61; 1964–65; 1968–69; 1973–76; 1979

CAREER HIGHLIGHTS: WWWF World Tag Team Champion (1973, w/Tony Garea); 2-time NWA Canadian Tag Team Champion (1966–68, w/Don Leo Jonathan)

FINISHING MANEUVER: Big Splash

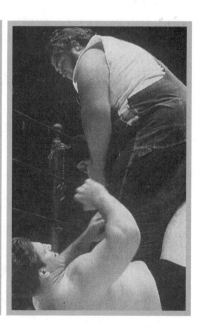

that changed fast. He grew to immense size early in life, and weighed in at 385 by the time he was eighteen. Attending high school in Pleasant Grove, Texas, he used his rapidly increasing size to his advantage on the football team, where he played defensive guard.

He had always been a wrestling fan, and when some wrestlers spotted him at a show once, they suggested he give the business a try. Wrestling promoters with dollar signs in their eyes recruited him to wrestle by the mid-1950s, when he was barely twenty years of age. In 1955, billed as Country Boy Calhoun, he had his first match in Kansas City, beating Lou Plummer.

Perhaps more than at any time before or since, pro wrestling in that era had a major element of the freak show to it, and Calhoun fit right in. At 601 pounds, he was among the most rotund grapplers anyone had ever seen, and that, combined with his country background, prompted Vincent J. McMahon in 1958 to nickname him "Haystacks." The hillbilly character he perfected, with T-shirt and overalls, and sporting a scruffy beard and horseshoe around his neck, has been copied many times by such performers as Hillbilly Jim and the Godwinns.

Calhoun was an instant hit among fans who clamored for the strange and bizarre; it didn't matter that his wrestling skill was limited. People came to see the spectacle of a man in wrestling territories across the nation. Much like Andre the Giant in later years, he was often brought into a territory for a limited time, to boost the magnitude of a particular card or add excitement to an ongoing feud. He would commonly remark, "There are going to be a lot of human pancakes around here before I get finished," and he usually made good on his promise.

Much like Andre the Giant, Calhoun too needed custom-made clothing, and even drove a custom-made ultrawide station wagon. In hotel rooms, he usually slept on the floor. In Boston, on one occasion, his weight caused an elevator he was riding in to fall.

As popular as he was with mat fans, Calhoun's fellow wrestlers sometimes found him egotistical and selfish, and believed he let his quick and easy fame go to his head. One particularly blunt viewpoint came from "Classy" Freddie Blassie, who wrote in his autobiography, *Listen, You Pencil Neck Geeks*:

"Calhoun was a freak, and the only reason he had a job was because he was so fuckin' big. He had no wrestling ability whatsoever, and never took the time to try and learn. He was an obnoxious bastard convinced that he was the number-one attraction in wrestling. I never heard anyone complain so much. He'd even complain about his complaints. When you wrestled him, you were limited because he couldn't do anything athletic. The only good thing about Calhoun was that he was an easy target when you were cutting a promo."

His colleagues' gripes notwithstanding, Calhoun may indeed have been one of the sport's hottest attractions. Fans instinctively took to his natural charisma in the ring, and found in him a kind of pathos that was irresistible. As unlikable as he may have been outside the ring, he was equally likable inside it. Known to his friends simply as "Stacks," he traveled wherever the money was, ensuring that neither he nor his 400-pound wife, Mary, would be missing any meals in the foreseeable future.

His size undoubtedly pushed him into the limelight faster than would have otherwise occurred, and on December 13, 1956, at the age of twenty-two, he challenged the great Lou Thesz for the NWA World Championship in Kansas City. Although he suffered a rare loss to the legendary Thesz, it was only the beginning of Calhoun's main-event days.

In the fall of 1958, Calhoun went to work for Vincent J. McMahon for the first time, during a period when McMahon's Capitol Wrestling Corporation (the future WWWF) was engaged in a war with the Buffalo promotion for control of the New York territory. Whether Calhoun helped tip the scales in McMahon's favor is debatable, but he certainly didn't hurt ticket sales.

He made his first Madison Square Garden appearance on September 17, thrashing thirty-year veteran "Judo" Jack Terry in under four minutes in the opening bout. (Terry would later become his business manager.) He quickly ascended to upper-midcard status, tangling with such foes as Karl Von Hess, the Miller

Haystacks Calhoun vs. "Judo" Jack Terry.

Brothers, and Johnny Valentine. On June 20, 1959, he attained his first main event in the wrestling mecca, battling NWA World Champion Pat O'Connor to a draw.

On May 21, 1960, Calhoun helped make the career of a young rookie named Bruno Sammartino. When the weightlifter-turned-wrestler was able to bodyslam and pin the gargantuan Calhoun in MSG, his reputation among fans was set for life, three years before he became World Champion.

Later that year, Calhoun began a memorable feud with U.S. Champion Buddy Rogers. It began when Haystacks, fed up with Rogers's underhanded tactics, interfered in the Nature Boy's tele-vised match with Abe Jacobs. The two met at the Garden in December 1960, and their war raged throughout the country, even after Rogers won the NWA World title in 1961. Rogers defended his crown against Haystacks in Boston in the fall of 1961 and Charlotte in the summer of 1962, winning by disqualification both times.

Stacks returned to WWWF after a brief hiatus in the fall of 1964. He formed a successful partnership with fellow fan favorite Bobo Brazil. It was also at this time that Calhoun entered into a titanic feud with the territory's other resident mastodon, the 401-pound Gorilla Monsoon. Battling throughout the area, Calhoun just barely settled the rivalry in his favor, and by the end of the summer of '65, he once again departed WWWF to tour the circuit.

He ventured through the Mid-South territory, where he held the NWA U.S. Tag Team title with a rookie Jack Brisco. In western Canada, he formed a Tag Team with another giant of the ring, Don Leo Jonathan. They held the NWA Canadian Tag Team title for a week in 1966. Two years later, Calhoun & Jonathan reunited to take the title back for a month.

By 1973, Haystacks Calhoun was not yet forty years old, but the stress put on his body by his obesity, not to mention the wear and tear of hauling his body around the ring, was taking its toll. He settled into WWWF for an extended run, and took a break from the relentless touring. In May he teamed up with Tony Garea, then a young newcomer, to take the World Tag Team Championship from Mr. Fuji & Professor Toru Tanaka in a match televised on *Championship Wrestling*. It was the biggest, and last, title he would ever hold.

"I enjoyed working with Haystacks," says Garea. "We never traveled together or socialized. I was young, and had things I wanted to do. I had to be in the gym every morning, and liked to go out and party at night. I was a smaller guy, the guy that found himself in trouble most of the time. I remember one time in Madison Square Garden, we were in a match that went thirty-three minutes, and I think I spent about twenty-seven of them in the ring! The fans wanted to see me get the big guy in, and that's what we did. He was the star of the team. Vince's father's thinking was, 'Garea's the rookie of the year, let's put him with Haystacks.' I think that helped me more than anything, when I look back now.

It was a great opportunity. Of course, Haystacks was a big man, so he never moved too fast. But he was very, very good with the fans. I thought we worked well as a team."

Fuji & Tanaka dogged the legend/rookie champions without mercy, finally regaining their gold in September. From there, Calhoun became a fixture on WWWF's weekly TV programs, squashing preliminary wrestlers, sometimes two at a time. His veteran status helped give a "rub" to popular stars he would team with, like Larry Zbysko and Chief Jay Strongbow. In late 1975, Calhoun went up against one of the company's hottest villains at the time, Ernie Ladd, and although Ladd wasn't able to beat Haystacks, he elevated his status by holding his own with him.

Calhoun went into semi-retirement in 1976. He made a brief comeback to the newly rechristened World Wrestling Federation three years later, giving one last rub to rookie sensation Steve Travis in a failed attempt to wrest the Tag Team title from Johnny & Jerry Valiant.

With the 1980s came a prolonged struggle with diabetes. Tragically, the disease led to the amputation of Calhoun's leg, after which he became a virtual recluse, gleaning whatever happiness he could from the fan letters that continued to roll in on a weekly basis. Finally, on December 7, 1989, William Calhoun passed away at North Texas Medical Center at just fifty-five years of age.

The legacy of Haystacks Calhoun is part of the legacy of the giant, an indispensable part of the sport dating back to its days as a carnival attraction. And although he may not have always been the most popular among his peers, there was no denying his unique connection with fans, who remembered him for his warmth, his charm, and his waistline.

- Just prior to the famous 1976 altercation between Gorilla Monsoon and Muhammad Ali, Monsoon's match opponent was Baron Scicluna.

- Scicluna's voice was permanently reduced to a whisper thanks to a kick to the throat from Emile Dupree (father of current Superstar Rene Dupree).

- Scicluna was trained alongside fellow WWWF legend Waldo Von Erich.

To younger fans who watched him in the late 1970s and early '80s, Baron Mikel Scicluna may seem to be little more than an opening-match preliminary wrestler. Yet those who go back further remember a different Baron, who headlined Madison Square Garden and was a leading Tag Team contender. Indeed, Scicluna's career in WWWF lasted long enough to encompass two entirely different periods, both of which are fondly remembered, for different reasons.

He was born Michael J. Scicluna in the Mediterranean island nation of Malta on July 29, 1929. He came to live in Toronto, Ontario, in 1950. Working out regularly at the local gym, he was exposed to the possibility of pro wrestling. Billed as Mike Valentino, he began his career working for Toronto promoter Frank Tunney in 1953.

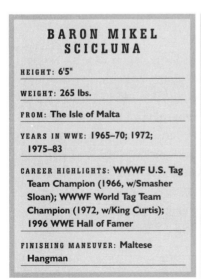

BARON MIKEL SCICLUNA

HEIGHT: 6'5"

WEIGHT: 265 lbs.

FROM: The Isle of Malta

YEARS IN WWE: 1965–70; 1972; 1975–83

CAREER HIGHLIGHTS: WWWF U.S. Tag Team Champion (1966, w/Smasher Sloan); WWWF World Tag Team Champion (1972, w/King Curtis); 1996 WWE Hall of Famer

FINISHING MANEUVER: Maltese Hangman

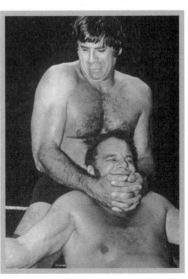

His size, particularly impressive for the period, made him an almost instant star, and he had his first match at the historic Maple Leaf Gardens in 1957. He became a challenger to Edouard Carpentier, recognized in many non-NWA territories as World Champion. It was also while competing in Canada that Scicluna would marry and have a son, Michael Jr.

WWWF owner Vince J. McMahon saw promise in the young giant. McMahon had a close working relationship with Tunney, and in 1965 he transformed Mike Valentino into Baron Mikel Scicluna and brought him to his northeastern territory. Inspired by 1950s California wrestler Baron Michele Leone, Scicluna came to the ring complete with a long red cape and other regal trappings.

He became known as the master of the foreign object, deftly finding hiding places for his dangerous weapons so the referee wouldn't detect them. It was usually a roll of coins, stashed in either his boot or his kneepad. Often, while being patted down before the bell, the Baron would hide the object on top of his head, much to the anger of the crowd.

He was catapulted right into a feud with WWWF Heavyweight Champion Bruno Sammartino, and challenged him at the Garden in two straight events in early 1966.

"Bruno was one of the best wrestlers I have ever seen in my life," says Scicluna. "A strongman who knew how to wrestle. I really enjoyed wrestling with Bruno."

By the fall, Scicluna had formed a Tag Team with the rugged Smasher Sloan. They defeated Johnny Valentine & Antonio Pugliese in September for the U.S. Tag Team title in a match made even more notable due to Valentine turning on his own partner. In December, Pugliese found a new partner in Spiros Arion, and joined forces with him to unseat Scicluna & Sloan.

Scicluna took a few months off from WWWF in 1968. After spending some time competing in Canada again, he headed to Australia, where he won the International Wrestling Alliance (IWA) Heavyweight title from old foe Spiros Arion and held it for three months.

After going back to work for McMahon, he challenged Sammartino once again in 1969 in a rare WWWF title match at the

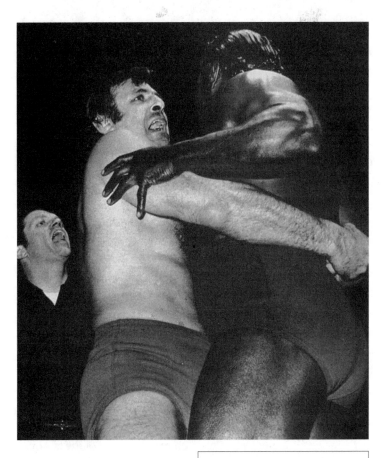

Baron Mikel Scicluna vs. Bobo Brazil.

Maple Leaf Gardens. He left in 1970 and was gone for the better part of two years.

At the beginning of 1972, he returned as a protégé of Capt. Lou Albano. Allying himself with King Curtis Iaukea, another Albano charge, Scicluna became half of the WWWF World Tag Team Champions after a victory over Karl Gotch & Rene Goulet in Philadelphia. In perhaps his WWWF highpoint, he battled Heavyweight Champion Pedro Morales in Madison Square Garden in March 1972, while holding Tag Team gold.

Just two months later, the Garden was the site of Scicluna's & Iaukea's loss of the Tag Team title to Chief Jay Strongbow & Sonny

King. The Baron disappeared from WWWF again almost immediately after.

The era of Baron Mikel Scicluna, top contender, was at an end. When he returned in the spring of 1975, something had changed. The middle-aged Scicluna's best days were behind him, and he became relegated to the role often given in those days to main-eventers past their prime. Competing mainly in lower-mid-card bouts, he would usually either lose to an up-and-coming Superstar or pull out an occasional win over another competitor also perennially stuck at the bottom of the card. Though unglamorous, it was an important role, as Scicluna was helping new competitors build their reputations.

"When you lose your title, you go down," he explains. "That's just how it is. I felt all right about it. I just kept in good shape, and kept at it."

Some may not have been able to stick around in such a role after having been a top star for the company. But Scicluna showed tremendous loyalty, loyalty that didn't go unnoticed. Occasionally, he would still find his way into a higher-profile match. He and Arion tried in vain to take the World Tag Team title from Tony Parisi (the former Pugliese) & Louis Cerdan in December '75; in March 1976, he squared off with former Olympic bronze medalist Chris Taylor; he battled Ivan Putski on the undercard of the famous June 1976 Shea Stadium show headlined by Sammartino vs. Stan Hansen and Muhammad Ali vs. Antonio Inoki.

The Baron remained a regular on nearly every major World Wrestling Federation live event and television taping right into the early 1980s. Finally, in 1983, years after his best days had gone, he called it quits and became a delivery-truck driver for the *New York Times*. He made one last return to the ring in 1987, competing in an old-timer's battle royal at the Meadowlands Arena in New Jersey. These days, a retired Mike Scicluna and his wife, Gloria, live in Pittsburgh, near their son Michael and their two grandsons.

Whether remembered as a towering threat to the Heavyweight Champion, or as a comical prelim act, Baron Scicluna remains a cult favorite among old-time fans. His years of service to the McMahons were rewarded with an induction into the WWE Hall of Fame in 1996.

- Steele played pro-wrestler-turned-actor Tor Johnson in the 1994 film *Ed Wood*.

- Steele is a member of the Michigan Coaches Hall of Fame.

- In a 1996 episode of *Seinfeld*, Jerry complained that his girlfriend had "man hands" that reminded him of George "The Animal" Steele.

WWE has always been known for its outlandish characters, and they didn't come any more outlandish and unpredictable than George "The Animal" Steele. A member of the WWE family on and off for more than three decades, Steele spanned the territorial WWWF era and the 1980s *Hulkamania* renaissance. Most amazingly of all, he did so while teaching high school in his native Detroit.

He was born William James Myers in the Motor City suburb of Madison Heights, Michigan, on April 16, 1937. In contrast to the animalistic character he would later portray, Jim Myers excelled in high school at both academics and athletics. He took part in basketball, baseball, and track, but it was football that was his

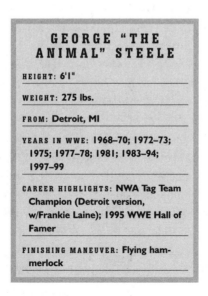

GEORGE "THE ANIMAL" STEELE

HEIGHT: 6'1"

WEIGHT: 275 lbs.

FROM: Detroit, MI

YEARS IN WWE: 1968–70; 1972–73; 1975; 1977–78; 1981; 1983–94; 1997–99

CAREER HIGHLIGHTS: **NWA Tag Team Champion (Detroit version, w/Frankie Laine); 1995 WWE Hall of Famer**

FINISHING MANEUVER: **Flying hammerlock**

great love. He attended Michigan State University, where he also played defensive tackle. Unfortunately, however, a blown knee ruined Myers's hopes of taking football beyond the college level.

By 1961, at twenty-four, Myers had already started a family. To support them, he went back to his old high school and took a position teaching gym and coaching the football team.

"That's all I ever wanted to do," he explains. "But at the time, I had two children and a third on the way, and I needed money."

Myers was pointed in the direction of Detroit promoter Bert Ruby. Thinking his athletic background would help get him noticed by the promoter, Myers never realized that it was something else altogether that would open the door.

"Bert took me into the back of his office and asked me to take off my shirt," he says. "He was looking for muscle tone and body build. But when he saw the hair on my body, he went, 'Wow!' He saw character. You see, I've always been hairy. I can remember going to the beach as a teenager, and hearing little kids say, 'Mommy, there's a gorilla over there.' It never really bothered me. I just laughed it off."

Now, Myers's hirsute body had become his ticket to wrestling stardom. He debuted under a mask as the villainous Student—an ironic moniker, considering his day job. In his first match, he was victorious over the veteran Klondike Bill in Kalamazoo.

During his time as the Student in Detroit, Myers was already learning the basics of being a wrestling villain. Among the tricks he picked up was something he'd carry with him through his whole career as "The Animal"—hiding foreign objects and then attacking his opponents with them when the referee wasn't looking, much to the dismay of the crowd that saw it all. Also while under the mask, Myers began making bizarre noises and awkward gestures to make up for the fact that fans couldn't see his face. These, too, would later become trademarks.

Myers's first love remained teaching his own students, and he therefore confined his wrestling exploits to the summer vacations. Sometimes, when he would take a rare wrestling date during the school year, he would drive one hundred and fifty miles to the arena after teaching a full day and overseeing football practice.

At the time, Pittsburgh was a satellite promotion of World Wide Wrestling Federation (WWWF), and it was there that Myers became George Steele, changing his name in part as a nod to Pittsburgh's primary industry. Taking off his mask, he exaggerated his unorthodox mannerisms and guttural noises even further, leading the fans to nickname him "The Animal."

In the summer of 1968, George "The Animal" Steele was invited by Vincent J. McMahon to work the main WWWF Northeast territory for the first time. He immediately became one of the most vicious and feared maniacs the promotion had ever seen. He opposed WWWF Heavyweight Champion Bruno Sammartino two months in a row at Madison Square Garden, and feuded with French Canadian legend Edouard Carpentier.

For nearly two decades, Steele would spend summers in WWWF, provoking terror from its fans and drawing blood from its heroes. Over time, he added more elements to his persona, such as the night in Pittsburgh when a fan threw a pillow at him and he bit it open, tossing the stuffing into the air.

"About two weeks later, I was wrestling Chief Jay Strongbow, and the match just sucked," he recalls. "So I looked at the turnbuckle and I said, 'I wonder . . .' It was one of those old Everlast turnbuckles, and when I took a bite out of it, it ripped like toilet paper. Out came the stuffing, and the place went nuts. So I started doing it almost every night."

In addition to the turnbuckle routine, Steele also became known for his green tongue—the result of consuming massive amounts of breath mints before each match.

The rumors ran rampant through the years about how Madison Heights' own Jim Myers was really George "The Animal" Steele. A popular urban legend of the day had it that the Animal was really a college professor of English.

Steele remained in constant contention for the Heavyweight title. He returned to challenge Sammartino in 1969 and 1975, as well as challenging other WWWF Heavyweight Champions such as

Pedro Morales (1972 and 1973) and Bob Backlund (1978, 1981, and 1983), and he was a thorn in the side of such popular favorites as Strongbow, Gorilla Monsoon, Tony Garea, and High Chief Peter Maivia.

By 1983, WWWF had become World Wrestling Federation, and Vincent J. McMahon had sold the company to his son, Vincent K. McMahon. Big changes were on the way, and both Steele and Vince's father felt that maybe it was time to let the Animal lumber off into the sunset.

"I had been there many years, and we had drawn a lot of money together, and had a lot of experiences," says Steele. "But he didn't want to see George 'The Animal' Steele become an old hang-around, and neither did I. We both had tears in our eyes, and we hugged. I finished up my matches, then got word that he had cancer. I called him a couple of times on the phone and told him what a great man he was, how much respect I had for him, how he'd helped my family and so on. And as far as I was concerned, when he died, the character known as George 'The Animal' Steele went into the coffin with him."

As it turned out, the following summer, he received a call from Vince Jr., who said he had a place for George Steele in his nationally expanding World Wrestling Federation. Beginning in the summer of 1984, Steele enjoyed a renaissance of his career that took him in a totally different direction. After being abandoned in the ring by tag team partners Nikolai Volkoff & the Iron Sheik, he started to gain the sympathy of the fans. By this point, he had adopted an even more "subhuman" persona, limiting his speech to simple words and phrases. As a result, Steele developed into one of the company's most beloved figures, a lonely, childlike brute who only wanted love.

Retiring from teaching in 1985, Steele began wrestling almost year-round. He engaged in what modern fans may remember as his most famous feud of all, with Randy "Macho Man" Savage, over the affections of his lovely manager, Elizabeth. Steele opposed Savage for the Intercontinental title at *WrestleMania 2*, and once even tried to kidnap Elizabeth, à la

King Kong and Fay Wray. The weird love triangle captured the hearts of fans completely.

"It was supposed to go on for three months," Steele reveals. "But the 'beauty and the beast' thing was so overwhelming that we ran with it for a long period of time."

But the in-ring career of the Animal was about to come to a forced end. Shortly after appearing in the battle royal at *WrestleMania IV*, he was diagnosed with Crohn's disease, a chronic inflammation of the small intestine. Retiring from competition, Steele was offered a job as a World Wrestling Federation road agent, a role that allowed him to impart what he knew to a new generation of Superstars. Although he held that position for several years, his heart was never quite in it. Still, he never forgot how the company threw him a lifeline when he was sick.

Relying on homeopathic treatments, Steele was able to successfully battle Crohn's disease, to the point that by 1998 doctors told him his condition was cured. Steele had improved to such a degree that at the age of sixty, he even returned to the ring for one last World Wrestling Federation run, as a member—appropriately enough—of the bizarre faction known as the Oddities. Ironically, his last major appearance was in WCW, where he defeated Jeff Jarrett on a 2000 episode of *WCW Monday Nitro*.

George "The Animal" Steele was a true WWE mainstay, one of those unique individuals, along with the likes of Gorilla Monsoon and Capt. Lou Albano, who spent almost his entire career in the Northeast. But that was not his only career. For as the man himself will tell you, Jim Myers and George Steele are two very different people.

AND THE LIST GOES
ON AND ON . . .

Needless to say, putting together a list of who to include in this book was no easy task, and I make no claim to be definitive. Along the way, a lot of very tough choices had to be made due to space limitations. To arrive at forty, some people simply had to be left out. Therefore, I've decided to cheat just a little bit (this is wrestling, after all—if the referee doesn't see it, it doesn't count, right?).

And so, I give you these additional WWE Legends. They may not have made the final cut, but this book would not be complete without them.

BOBBY DAVIS. Before there was Bobby Heenan, or even Capt. Lou Albano, there was Bobby Davis, the original manager of champions. An obnoxious Elvis knockoff with slick black hair and sequined jackets, his greatest claim to fame was being the manager of Buddy Rogers. Also on his client list were the Graham Brothers and "Cowboy" Bob Orton Sr.

"CRAZY" LUKE GRAHAM. The third Graham brother, Crazy Luke was originally a replacement for Eddie Graham, but came into his own in the late 1960s and '70s. He was U.S. Tag Team Champion with Dr. Jerry Graham, and in 1971 joined forces with

Tarzan Tyler under the management of Lou Albano to become WWWF's first World Tag Team Champions.

DOMINIC DENUCCI. This native of Campo Baso, Italy, was a company mainstay from the late 1960s to the early '80s, a regular on virtually every weekly TV broadcast. He was a frequent Tag Team partner to Bruno Sammartino and held the World Tag Team title with Victor Rivera, Irish Pat Barrett, and Dino Bravo. In later years, he trained individuals like Shane Douglas and Mick Foley for the ring. He currently resides in Pittsburgh.

DON LEO JONATHAN. The "Mormon Giant," Don Leo Jonathan was one of the most agile big men to ever set foot in the ring. Before he "passed the torch" to Andre the Giant, the massive Jonathan was a top challenger to Bruno Sammartino during Bruno's second Heavyweight title reign. In later years, he focused on deep-sea diving and an underwater mining business. As a rookie, Jonathan was traveling with Jess McMahon when the McMahon patriarch passed away in 1954.

THE FABULOUS KANGAROOS. Al Costello & Roy Heffernan, the original Fabulous Kangaroos, made up one of the top duos of the late 1950s and early '60s, second only to the Graham Brothers among heel tandems. Known for the boomerangs that both represented their native Australia and served as convenient foreign objects, the Kangaroos were three-time U.S. Tag Team Champions.

JOHNNY RODZ. Born and bred in Brooklyn, "The Unpredictable" Johnny Rodz gave his all each and every time he got in the ring. He could always be counted on to have a great match, even if he didn't always win. His years of loyalty through the 1960s, '70s, and '80s earned him an induction to the WWE Hall of Fame. Training wrestlers out of the world-famous Gleason's Gym for more than twenty years, he produced such athletes as Tazz and Tommy Dreamer.

MIGUEL PEREZ. Best known as the longtime Tag Team partner of Antonino Rocca, Puerto Rican Superstar Miguel Perez was immensely popular during the late 1950s and early '60s, and continued to compete in WWWF for years after Rocca departed in 1963. His son, Miguel Perez Jr., was a member of the Los Boricuas faction in World Wrestling Federation during the late 1990s. Perez died in 2005.

PROFESSOR TORU TANAKA. The good professor formed one of the longest-running Tag Team partnerships of all time with the devious Mr. Fuji during the 1970s. They held the WWWF World Tag Team title a record-setting three times, and also found great success in many diverse territories. Earlier in his career, Tanaka teamed with Mitsu Arakawa to win the WWWF International Tag Team title as the Rising Suns. Tanaka also challenged Bruno Sammartino in the main event of the last event held at the old Madison Square Garden. In later years, he made frequent appearances in movies, commercials, and music videos.

SPIROS ARION. Continuing a tradition of Greek wrestlers that stretched all the way back to the great Jim Londos, Spiros Arion was a top competitor of the 1960s and '70s. First introduced as a popular favorite in 1965, he made a famous turn to the dark side during his second run in the mid-1970s. Fans still talk about his vicious betrayal of former Tag Team partner Chief Jay Strongbow, who had his ceremonial headdress shoved in his mouth by Arion. Later, Arion challenged Bruno Sammartino in the most heated feud of 1975.

STAN HANSEN. Master of the brutal lariat clothesline, Stan Hansen was a rough-and-tumble customer from Borger, Texas, who shocked the wrestling world in 1976 when he broke the neck of Bruno Sammartino with his crippling finisher. The two later met in a showdown at Shea Stadium that many consider the greatest match of Bruno's career. After leaving WWWF, Hansen spent the bulk of his career in Japan, where he became arguably the most successful American wrestler in that nation's history.

STAN STASIAK. Often overlooked when the catalogue of WWE Champions is tallied, Stan "The Man" Stasiak nevertheless was a holder of the title, and played an integral part in its history. Specifically, he was the bridge between the reign of Pedro Morales, which he ended on December 1, 1973, and the second reign of

Bruno Sammartino, who defeated him for the gold on December 10, 1973. Although only the champ for a mere nine days, Stasiak was before and after a rugged, formidable bruiser.

TONY ATLAS. Known as "Mr. USA," Tony Atlas possessed one of the most finely honed physiques the sport of kings has ever seen. A man of great strength and conditioning, he was a popular Superstar of the early 1980s who went on to become one-half of the game's first black World Tag Team Champions with Rocky Johnson. He is also one of a handful of competitors who can boast a pinfall victory over Hulk Hogan in WWE.

WALDO VON ERICH. Billed as the cousin of Fritz Von Erich, Waldo Von Erich was WWWF's resident goose-stepping Nazi villain, coming to the ring in full regalia and drawing serious heat from the crowd whenever he did so. No other opponent challenged Bruno Sammartino as many times as Von Erich, who faced the champion in seven different main events at Madison Square Garden alone between 1964 and 1975.

"WILD RED" BERRY. A standout junior heavyweight wrestler of the 1930s and '40s, Fred "Wild Red" Berry transitioned successfully into the managerial end of the business, becoming one of WWWF's top two managers (along with Bobby Davis) during much of the 1960s. He brought Gorilla Monsoon to the territory in 1959, and also led the Fabulous Kangaroos to great success. Fred Berry passed away in 1973.

And last but not least . . .

LITTLE PEOPLE. Midget wrestlers were long a staple of pro wrestling shows, but nowhere else were they as popular as in the Northeast, where they enjoyed a spot on nearly every card. In fact, the first show put on at Madison Square Garden by Vincent J. McMahon was also the first Garden show to feature midgets. Many came and went, but three stood out as the greatest of them all: **Sky Lo Lo, Little Beaver,** and **Lord Littlebrook.** Sky Lo Lo was perhaps the most prolific, at one time boasting the Midget World Championship, and competing from the 1940s well into the

1980s. The Montreal legend died in 1998. Little Beaver was an extremely popular Native American performer whose career ranged from the 1960s into the *Hulkamania* era of the 1980s. In fact, he participated in a Mixed Tag Team match at *WrestleMania III* in 1987. He died in 1995. Also featured in that *WrestleMania III* match was Lord Littlebrook, a prominent British midget competitor who captured the Midget World Championship in the early 1970s. In later years, he trained a new generation of little people to carry on this dying subgenre of the sport.

A LEGENDS LIBRARY

Here's a list of some of the books and films that proved so very valuable in researching the information that went into this book:

Albano, Capt. Lou, Bert Randolph Sugar, and Roger Woodson. *The Complete Idiot's Guide to Pro Wrestling*. New York: Alpha Books, 1999.

Blassie, "Classy" Freddie, with Keith Elliot Greenberg. *Listen, You Pencil Neck Geeks*. New York: Pocket Books, 2003.

Boesch, Paul. *Hey Boy! Where'd You Get Them Ears?: 55 Years of Pro Wrestling*. Edited by J. Michael Kenyon. Houston: Minuteman Press Southwest, 2000.

Bruno Sammartino: Strongman. TV special. Directed by George Romero. Pittsburgh: Laurel Sports, 1975.

Duncan, Royal, and Gary Will. *Wrestling Title Histories*. Waterloo, Ontario: Archeus Communications, 2000.

Ellison, Lillian, with Larry Platt. *The Fabulous Moolah: First Goddess of the Squared Circle*. New York: ReganBooks, 2002.

Foley, Mick. *Have a Nice Day! A Tale of Blood and Sweatsocks*. New York: ReganBooks, 1999.

Griffin, Marcus. *Fall Guys: The Barnums of Bounce*. Chicago: Reilly & Lee, 1937. Reprint, Hendersonville, Tenn.: Scott Teal, 1997.

Heenan, Bobby, with Steve Anderson. *Bobby the Brain: Wrestling's Bad Boy Tells All*. Chicago: Triumph Books, 2002.

Jares, Joe. *Whatever Happened to Gorgeous George?* Englewood Cliffs, N.J.: Prentice-Hall, 1974.

Lentz, Harris M. III. *Biographical Dictionary of Professional Wrestling.* Jefferson, N.C.: McFarland & Co., 1997.

Lewin, Ted. *I Was a Teenage Professional Wrestler.* New York: Scholastic, 1993.

London Publishing Company. *The 1999 Wrestling Almanac and Book of Facts.* Fort Washington, Penn.: London Publishing, 1999.

Meltzer, Dave. *Tributes: Remembering Some of the World's Greatest Wrestlers.* Etobicoke, Ontario: Winding Stair Press, 2001.

ACKNOWLEDGMENTS

First and foremost, I'd like to thank my whole family for inspiring me to take on this project and see it through. In particular, heaps of gratitude go to my main sources of inspiration: my amazing wife, Philana, who's been putting up with this whole wrestling thing for thirteen years now, and our beautiful kids, Layla and Jack (my real bosses).

WWE Legends would not have been nearly as thorough as it is were it not for the extended interview granted to me by Vince McMahon, an interview that turned out to be the cornerstone of the whole book. My thanks also go to Beth Zazza for making that interview possible.

I am grateful to Stacey Pascarella for helping to get the ball rolling on the *WWE Legends* project, as well as to Dean Miller for following it through to the finish line. My thanks go to the members of WWE's Publications department (past and present) who have groomed me as a writer for the past six years, and who permitted me to quote from the many articles we've published in *Raw* and *SmackDown!* magazines on the legends of the business.

I'm thankful to Simon & Schuster for taking a chance on a book like this. Special thanks to Margaret Clark for being the most helpful editor a first-time author could hope for over the course of the three years that *WWE Legends* has been in the works.

Major thanks go to London Publishing for providing all the photos for this book, the majority of the content of which predates WWE's own photo archive. And we wouldn't have been able to select and acquire those photos without the help of Noelle Carr and Frank Vitucci of WWE's photography department.

It was a dream come true to have the one and only Sgt. Slaughter—a true WWE legend if ever there was one—write the foreword to this book. I never even imagined he'd be able to make the time for it at all, let alone contribute something as moving and insightful as he did.

To the legends who actually sat down to be interviewed specifically for this book, I am eternally grateful—especially Superstar Billy Graham, Arnold Skaaland, Tony Garea, Baron Mikel Scicluna, and of course, Sarge. I also want to acknowledge those other luminaries who gave their valuable insight, such as "Nature Boy" Ric Flair, Ricky "The Dragon" Steamboat, "Mean" Gene Okerlund, Chris Nowinski, and the dean of referees, Dick Kroll.

To those who helped out in so many ways, thank you: to Aaron "Double" Feigenbaum for giving me access to some previously recorded interviews, as well as Phil Speer and especially Keith Elliot Greenberg for allowing me to quote from their work. And to my best pal, Chris Mari, for his valuable insight on the manuscript, and for listening to me wax rhapsodic on the virtues of Toots Mondt and "Classy" Freddie Blassie.

INDEX